JEAN ANOUILH

Antigone

translated by
BARBARA BRAY
with commentary and notes by
TED FREEMAN

Bloomsbury Methuen Drama
An imprint of Bloomsbury Publishing Plc

B L O O M S B U R Y
LONDON · OXFORD · NEW YORK · NEW DELHI · SYDNEY

Bloomsbury Methuen Drama

An imprint of Bloomsbury Publishing Plc

Imprint previously known as Methuen Drama

50 Bedford Square	1385 Broadway
London	New York
WC1B 3DP	NY 10018
UK	USA

www.bloomsbury.com

**BLOOMSBURY, METHUEN DRAMA and the
Diana logo are trademarks of Bloomsbury Publishing Plc**

This edition first published in the United Kingdom in 2000 by
Methuen Publishing Ltd
Reissued with additional material and a new cover design 2005;
with a new cover design 2009
Antigone first published in 1987 by
Methuen Drama in *Anouilh Plays: One*
Reprinted by Bloomsbury Methuen Drama 2013, 2014, 2015 (twice), 2016 (twice)

British Library Cataloguing-in-Publication Data
A catalogue record for this book is available from the British Library.

ISBN: PB: 978-0-4136-9540-6
ePDF: 978-1-4081-7147-9
ePub: 978-1-4081-6991-9

Library of Congress Cataloging-in-Publication Data
A catalog record for this book is available from the Library of Congress.

Series: Student Editions

Typeset by Deltatype Ltd, Birkenhead, Merseyside
Printed and bound in Great Britain

Contents

Jean Anouilh:
1910–1987

Few twentieth-century French authors were more
unwilling than Jean Anouilh to talk or write about his
private life; he always considered such matters to be no
business of students and teachers of his work. In 1946,
however, in a letter to the critic Hubert Gignoux, Anouilh
parted with a few facts about his early years. These were
supplemented in 1987 by his 'Souvenirs' bearing the
whimsical title *La Vicomtesse d'Eristal n'a pas reçu son balai
mécanique* ('The Viscountess d'Eristal Has Not Received
Her Mechanical Carpet-Sweeper') which, we are
encouraged to believe, is the exact wording of the first
complaint he had to field in his first job in a Paris
department store.

Once Anouilh's early years are left behind, this
chronology is mainly a list of his achievements in the
theatre, consisting of the dates of the first performances of
his better-known plays. The listing is not intended to be
exhaustive, as it would extend to well over sixty items if his
translations and adaptations (e.g. of Shakespeare) were
included, not to mention his film scenarios.

One of the dramatists admired by Anouilh was George
Bernard Shaw and he adopted his way of classifying his
plays, along the lines of the 'Plays Pleasant' and 'Plays
Unpleasant', but dividing them into categories. When
Anouilh's plays were first published in collected volumes,
he grouped them into:

Pièces noires (Balzac, Paris, 1942) – 'Black Plays'
Pièces roses (Balzac, 1942) – 'Pink Plays'
Nouvelles Pièces noires (La Table Ronde, Paris, 1946) –
    'More Black Plays'
Pièces brillantes (La Table Ronde, 1951) – 'Glittering Plays'
Pièces grinçantes (La Table Ronde, 1958) – 'Grating Plays'

Pièces costumées (La Table Ronde, 1960) – 'Plays in
  Costume'
Nouvelles Pièces grinçantes (La Table Ronde, 1970) – 'More
  Grating Plays'
Pièces baroques (La Table Ronde, 1974) – 'Baroque Plays'

Much of the time the classification is rather arbitrary;
more than one critic has made the point that *grinçant* is the
most appropriate category: all of Anouilh's plays are in
some measure 'grating'.

1910 Jean Anouilh is born on 23 June in Bordeaux. His
     father François Anouilh is a tailor, his mother Marie-
     Magdalène a violinist in the casino orchestra in the
     nearby resort of Arcachon. As a small boy in this
     environment, Jean becomes familiar with the world
     of light music and operetta. The milieu of rank and
     file musicians and performers, eking out a penurious
     living in mediocre provincial tours or 'engagements
     for the season', will be used as a setting for certain of
     his plays.
1918 The family moves to Paris, where Anouilh's father
     finds work as a tailor's cutter. From his earliest years
     Jean is fascinated by the theatre, and writes youthful
     efforts in the manner of Molière and Edmond
     Rostand whose *Cyrano de Bergerac* had been one of
     the great successes at the turn of the century.
     Throughout his teens Jean sees plays performed
     professionally in Paris whenever possible.
1927 Jean finishes his secondary education at the Collège
     (now Lycée) Chaptal, where a classmate is Jean-
     Louis Barrault, destined to become one of France's
     greatest theatre directors. Enrols at the Sorbonne to
     study law ('what people study in France for want of
     a better idea'), but soon gives up, being more and
     more determined to become a dramatist. One of his
     favourite contemporary directors is Charles Dullin, a
     champion of the Italian dramatist Luigi Pirandello.
     The influence of the 'Sicilian magician' on Anouilh's
     dramatic craftsmanship and whole conception of the

theatre will be striking.

1928 An equally important influence is that of Jean Giraudoux, whose first play *Siegfried*, is directed at the Théâtre des Champs-Élysées by another leading director of the era, Louis Jouvet. This event is considered to be one of the defining moments in the renaissance of the French theatre in the twentieth century.

1929 Anouilh's first professional experience, secretary to Jouvet, proves not to be congenial. The two do not get on, although according to legend Jouvet later lends the hard-up Anouilh some of the set furniture from *Siegfried* to furnish his flat when, in 1932 . . .

1932 . . . Anouilh marries the actress Monelle Valentin who will play the lead in three of his plays ten years later. The first production of one of his plays, *L'Hermine* (*Pièces noires*, *The Ermine*), is given thirty-seven performances at the Théâtre de l'Oeuvre - 'from this moment I made my mind up to live from writing for the theatre'. It is typical of Anouilh's 'Black Plays' in the 1930s in its naturalist style and bleak message: young love cannot survive poverty and the compromises necessary in adult life.

1933 Daughter Catherine is born.

1934 *Y avait un prisonnier* (There Was a Prisoner) is performed fifty times at the Théâtre des Ambassadeurs. Metro-Goldwyn-Mayer buys the film rights: the Anouilh couple's finances improve greatly. However, the film is not made; the play is never included by the author in his collected volumes.

1937 *Voyageur sans bagage* (*Pièces noires*, *Traveller without Luggage*) is directed by one of Anouilh's idols, Georges Pitoëff, and runs for one hundred and ninety performances at the Théâtre des Mathurins.

1938 *La Sauvage* (*Pièces noires*, *Restless Heart*) is directed by Pitoëff at the Mathurins. In September *Le Bal des voleurs* (*Pièces roses*, *Thieves' Carnival*) is directed by the man who will be Anouilh's first-choice director for the next ten years, André Barsacq, and has two hundred performances. It has incidental music by Darius Milhaud. Anouilh is beginning to make his mark.

1939 Anouilh is drafted into the French army and briefly made a prisoner of war when France surrenders to Germany in 1940. He exploits an administrative error to 'demobilise' himself and make his way back to Paris where he stays throughout the Occupation, making his living from the theatre.

1940 *Léocadia* (*Pièces roses*) runs for one hundred and fifty performances at the Théâtre de la Michodière, directed by the leading film actor Pierre Fresnay, with music by Francis Poulenc.

1941 *Le Rendez-vous de Senlis* (*Pièces roses, Dinner with the Family*) directed by Barsacq at the Théâtre de l'Atelier.

1942 *Eurydice* (*Pièces noires, Point of Departure,* also known as *Legend of Lovers*) directed by Barsacq at the Atelier (ninety performances).

1944 (February) *Antigone* (*Nouvelles Pièces noires*) begins a run of five hundred performances at the Atelier, directed by Barsacq, with Monelle Valentin in the leading role. Unlike the two previous productions, *Antigone* and *Eurydice* are the first of the plays performed during the Second World War to have been written during it. The choice of an ancient mythic theme ending inevitably in death reflects an intense mood of despair in the author as a result of the nation's experiences at this time.

1945 Despite the relative affluence which an annual succession of long runs of his plays now brings, Anouilh continues to experience personal unhappiness at the Liberation. His marriage to Monelle Valentin begins to unravel, and his perception of modern French political and social values undergoes a profound shock in the immediate

aftermath of the defeat of the Nazis and their
Vichyite collaborators. On 6 February the anti-
semitic journalist and intellectual Raymond
Brasillach is executed by firing squad, having been
tried and convicted in the course of the official
purges (*épuration*). Despite being only vaguely
acquainted with him, Anouilh is involved in a last-
minute campaign to save Brasillach from execution.
He and other writers attempt to persuade colleagues
to sign a petition for a plea of clemency; many refuse
to sign. General de Gaulle, head of the provisional
government, turns down the plea; he is henceforth
bitterly detested by Anouilh. As a result of this
campaign, Anouilh is further suspect in the eyes of
left-wing intellectuals and critics: their interpretation
of *Antigone* as more an apologia for Pétain and Vichy
than an endorsement of resistance to tyranny is now
reinforced.

1947 *L'Invitation au château* (*Pièces brillantes, Ring Round
the Moon*) produced at the Atelier, music by Poulenc
(three hundred and thirty-four performances).

1948 *Ardèle* (*Pièces grinçantes*) performed at the Comédie
des Champs-Elysées.

1949 Successful production of *Antigone* at the London Old
Vic, starring Laurence Olivier (Prologue-Chorus),
Vivien Leigh (Antigone), and George Relph
(Creon).

1950 *La Répétition ou l'amour puni* (*Pièces brillantes, The
Rehearsal*) directed by Jean-Louis Barrault at the
Théâtre Marigny.

1951 *Colombe* (*Pièces brillantes*) directed by Barsacq at the
Atelier.

1952 *La Valse des toréadors* (*Pièces grinçantes, Waltz of the
Toreadors*) performed at the Comédie des Champs-
Elysées, directed by Jean-Denis Malclès, normally
until now Anouilh's designer. Mixed reception (two
hundred performances).

1953 Anouilh divorces Monelle Valentin, marries the

actress Nicole Lançon, future mother of Caroline,
Marie-Colombe and Nicolas. Failure of *Médée*
(*Nouvelles Pièces noires*, *Medea*, written 1946) after
only thirty-two performances, directed at the Atelier
by Barsacq (his last production for Anouilh).
L'Alouette (*Pièces costumées*, *The Lark*), begins a run
of over six hundred performances at the Théâtre
Montparnasse, directed by Anouilh and Roland
Pietri.

1956 *Pauvre Bitos* (*Pièces grinçantes*, *Poor Bitos*) begins a
long controversial run at the Théâtre Montparnasse.
The play is perceived to be a reactionary
interpretation of the post-Second World War purges
of collaborators and the execution of Robert
Brasillach, whom Anouilh had defended in vain.
Increasingly Anouilh and his new family are absent
from Paris; they eventually settle for the last thirty
years of his life near Lausanne on the shores of Lake
Geneva.

1959 *Becket, ou l'honneur de Dieu* (*Pièces costumées*, *Becket,
or the Honour of God*) begins a run of six hundred
performances at the Théâtre Montparnasse,
directed by Anouilh and Pietri.

1961 *La Grotte* (*Pièces grinçantes*, *The Cavern*) opens at the
Théâtre Montparnasse. The production team is
now established more or less for the remainder of
Anouilh's career: himself and Pietri directing, Jean-
Denis Malclès designing décor and costumes.
During the sixties Anouilh becomes increasingly
jaundiced about contemporary French society; he
loathes De Gaulle who is now back in power, but
detests the far left militant opposition to him even
more. Also, he resents attacks upon his plays by the
younger generation of critics and the champions of
the absurdist avant-garde, despite the fact that he
has given enthusiastic support to early plays by
Beckett and Ionesco. He goes through a phase of
adapting and directing work by dramatists he

admires such as Shakespeare, Kleist, Vitrac.

1968 *Le Boulanger, la boulangère et le petit mitron* (*Pièces grinçantes*, The Baker, the Baker's Wife and the Little Baker's Boy), the first of the dozen or so plays that make up the last phase of Anouilh's writing career. It runs for one hundred and seventy-three performances at the grand Right Bank theatre, the Comédie des Champs-Elysées, which is increasingly his spiritual home.

1969 *Cher Antoine, ou l'Amour Raté* (*Pièces baroques*, Dear Antoine, or Love's Failure) begins a run of three hundred and seventeen performances. The mood is as 'grating' as that of the previous play and all those to follow, many of which will continue to be designated '*grinçant*' and also deal with the tribulations of anyone enmeshed in the traditional family unit. But *Cher Antoine*'s new category, '*baroque*', which it shares with *Ne Réveillez pas Madame* (Don't Wake Madame; 1970) and *Le Directeur de l'Opéra* (The Director of the Opera; 1972), announces a renewed flourish of dazzling theatricality. Anouilh leads us through a labyrinthine journey into the past of a central male protagonist, often a successful author or theatre director in late middle age, much plagued by personal and family problems, income tax demands, jealous rivals, hostile critics, etc., an author not unlike Jean Anouilh at this late stage of his career. Despite the baroque and brilliant stagecraft, the mood is as 'black' and 'grating' as it was at the time of *Antigone*. But youth is no longer sacrosanct. The teenage daughter, as in *Les Poissons rouges* (The Goldfish; 1970), is now likely to be pregnant, fired up on feminist theory, and cursing her father for being a failed human being, the source of all the family's woes.

1987 Anouilh dies of a heart attack on 3 October in Lausanne.

Plot

The play is not divided into scenes or acts, and is performed without an interval.

At the opening curtain we see a 'neutral' set – one which can be anywhere at any time. All the characters are on stage, waiting to be presented. This is done by the Prologue, who comes to the front of the stage to describe the characters in turn, outline the plot, and above all set the mood for the play. The plot and characterisation are similar to those of Sophocles' *Antigone*. The one change of some significance is that Anouilh has completely omitted the prophet Tiresias (this is one of the ways in which he switches the focus in the play more towards the heroine and away from Creon than did Sophocles). Also, despite the prescribed 'neutral' setting, there are other subtle differences of emphasis and modernising features. The costumes are contemporary with the period of the production; the Prologue's presentation contains a number of other anachronisms: the waiting characters are 'playing cards, knitting, and so on'; Haemon has asked Antigone to marry him at a ball; in happier times Creon likes strolling around town inspecting antique shops.

The Prologue comments that certain characters – or, to use the nuance borrowed from Pirandello, actors waiting to become the characters – look more solemn than others, as they know what lies ahead. Antigone is destined to die young, without marrying her fiancé Haemon. She will be condemned to death by her uncle Creon, king of Thebes and Haemon's father. Her crime is to be that of disobeying Creon's order to leave the corpse of her brother Polynices to rot outside the city

walls and be fought over by birds and jackals. He and
his brother Eteocles had been killed in their internecine
struggle to become sole ruler of Thebes. Having been
described, the characters leave the stage in turn. The
action begins as the Prologue repeats the warning of
the edict: 'Anyone affording Polynices proper burial
rites will be mercilessly punished, with death.'

The light changes; it is a 'grey dawn in a sleeping
house' as Antigone comes into the house carrying her
shoes. She is challenged by the nurse and explains that
she has been out for a walk to see the dawn. Antigone
at first allows the nurse to believe that she has been out
for a romantic rendezvous. As Antigone is engaged to
Haemon, the nurse is scandalised, but before she can
get at the truth Antigone's sister Ismene enters. The
nurse is hustled out to make breakfast for the
princesses. Ismene confesses to her sister that she is not
courageous enough to support Antigone in giving their
brother a decent burial. The difference of character
between the sisters is apparent. Ismene has always been
a conformist and respecter of authority; she can
sympathise with Creon in that his edict has been forced
upon him solely by the need to quell anarchy in
Thebes. Antigone has always been a rebel, impulsive
and passionate, and a tomboy bitterly resentful at
being, in Ismene's words, 'only a girl'. With their
difference of opinion unresolved about covering up the
corpse of Polynices, Ismene goes off to bed as the
nurse returns. In the sentimental scene that follows,
Antigone recalls her not so distant childhood memories
of being comforted by the nurse. The latter is happy to
play this role again but is bewildered as to why
Antigone hints at a looming event, as a result of which,
for example, it might be necessary to take special care
of her pet dog.

It is then Haemon's turn to be alarmed and
bewildered by Antigone's dramatic warning that their
dreams of marrying and having a son will come to

nothing. He is 'dumbfounded', but she makes him leave without questioning her. Ismene enters briefly to plead with Antigone not to make a nocturnal visit to the corpse. The latter replies with 'a strange smile' that it is too late to abandon her plan: that was where she had been when she met Ismene at dawn. With this *coup de théâtre*, Antigone briskly exits, with Ismene running after her.

Although Anouilh indicates no interval nor even a new act, there is effectively a major break at this point. Creon enters with his page, and has Private Jonas brought in, one of the three soldiers who have been guarding the corpse of Polynices. Jonas is 'green with fear', having drawn the short straw to bring a confidential message to Creon: during the night someone has covered the corpse with soil. All that is known is that it is someone who made a light footprint and left behind a child's spade. Creon is furious and suspects political elements in the strife-torn state, using a child for the task in order to make a propaganda coup if the child is caught. The panic-stricken Jonas is ordered to make sure that the incident is hushed up, or else he and his colleagues will die.

The Prologue-Chorus now enters to deliver a soliloquy. The tragedy that is about to unfold is inevitable. It is like a tensed spring or a finely tuned machine ready to be put in motion 'at the flick of a finger'. Everything will now go off like clockwork, right up to the moment when the executioner's arm is raised in the last act with the crowd watching. Whereas in melodrama there is always the hope of being saved, in tragedy there is no 'lousy hope', you are caught like a rat in a trap. You can shout till your lungs burst, but to no avail. Tragedy is gratuitous, pointless, irremediable. Antigone is now dragged in by the guards, having been caught trying to cover up the body. The Chorus exits with the observation that the time has come for her 'to be herself at last'.

Jonas and his colleagues Snout and Binns are
exultant, as they assume they're going to be rewarded.
Perhaps they'll get a cash bonus, enough to go out on
a spree without their wives knowing? When Antigone
tells them she is the daughter of Oedipus, they laugh:
she is just like those tarts who always claim to be the
police chief's girlfriend when they are arrested at night.
Creon enters and is incredulous when he discovers who
the culprit is. Antigone is unrepentant. She confirms
the guards' report. Creon dismisses them with strict
instructions to tell no one about what has happened.
He still hopes the matter can be hushed up.

The scene that follows is by far the longest and most
famous in the play. Creon the 'realist', the desperate
ruler of a dangerously anarchic state, is confronted with
Antigone the 'idealist'. The daughter of the proud and
headstrong Oedipus is resolved to give Polynices proper
burial rites simply because he was her brother, despite
the fact that he was a traitor. She does not care either
that the consequences for herself will certainly be death
– not for one second does she expect her royal status
to protect her. In despair, Creon deploys a variety of
arguments to try to persuade her to be reasonable, but
she stubbornly persists. She knows that her gesture is
meaningless in practical terms and if he wishes to
prevent her from repeating it, he will have to put her to
death: 'I'm not here to understand. I'm here to say no
to you, and to die.' Creon argues that he too would
have liked to say no to the odious task of re-
establishing order in Thebes, but it would have been
irresponsible: somebody had to have the courage to
do it.

Reasoning with Antigone is futile. It is at this point
that Creon appears to hit upon a winning strategy,
telling her the truth about Eteocles and Polynices. The
two brothers whom she worshipped when she was a
little girl were in fact monsters. While still an
adolescent, Polynices was a loutish drunkard, a

spendthrift who once struck his father Oedipus full in
the face for refusing to pay his gambling debts. When
he left home he sided with the Argives and plotted to
kill his father. Antigone is seriously affected by this
discovery; worse is to come. Creon tells her what only
he knows: Eteocles was no better – every bit as
treacherous and eager to kill his father as was
Polynices. It is not even certain that the corpse that lies
in the state hero's tomb is his, so badly mangled were
both bodies in the fratricidal combat. For political
purposes one brother had to be declared a hero, the
other a traitor. Antigone is crushed, and at first accepts
Creon's recommendation: comply, survive, marry
Haemon.

Creon now makes a serious mistake. He
philosophises about the importance of accepting life in
all its complexity: what anyone learns on growing older
is that despite its imperfection and disappointments life
can still offer *happiness*. This is the fatal word. Antigone
wakes as if from a trance, and explodes in a tirade of
contempt for all who accept that this conception of
happiness can compensate for the dwindling of the
fierce ideals – and physical perfection – of youth. She
wants everything or nothing, and it must always be as
wonderful as it was when she was little. At the height
of the row, with Antigone screaming insults at Creon,
Ismene enters. She assures Antigone that she is now
willing to help her bury Polynices, but her offer is
angrily rejected. Creon acknowledges defeat and
summons the guards to take Antigone away. As she is
dragged off, she cries out, *in relief*, 'At last, Creon! At
last!'

From this point on the rhythm of the play reminds
us of the Chorus's metaphor earlier. The tensed spring
has been released, the machine is in operation and the
tragedy grinds to its inevitable conclusion. There can
still be surprises but only minor ones; Antigone is
doomed.

The Chorus is now alone briefly with Creon, pleading with him to spare Antigone but disarmed in the face of the latter's argument that she was determined to die. Polynices was just a pretext; when that was invalid, another reason was immediately found. Haemon bursts in to plead in turn with his father, only to be told that if Antigone loved him she would have agreed to live. A moving scene ensues between the two men in which Creon tries to convince Haemon that every young man sooner or later has to realise that he has 'looked up' to his father too long. To be a man is to know that 'we are alone. The world is empty'. Haemon exits in despair, crying out Antigone's name. Creon goes out with the guards to organise the defence of the palace against the infuriated mob.

Antigone is left alone with the guard Jonas, while waiting to be taken off to execution. It is a long scene, semi-comic at first, as Jonas rambles on about the pros and cons of a career as a guardsman – pay, conditions, status, etc. – compared with being a sergeant in the regular army. In reply to her enquiry, he informs Antigone that she is to die by being immured in a cave outside the city – no doubt another hot and thankless task that will fall to the guards as usual . . . In return for the offer of Antigone's gold ring he nervously agrees to deliver a message to Haemon, which she dictates to him. She almost ends her letter by confessing what she now realises: it would have been easy to agree to live; she is afraid and does not know what she is dying for. But she thinks better of it; 'I'm sorry' will do instead. 'Funny sort of letter,' concludes Jonas, pocketing the ring as his colleagues enter to take Antigone off to her death.

The Chorus observes that Antigone's fate is decided and it is now the turn of everyone else to suffer. Creon's ordeal is recounted to the Chorus by the messenger. Haemon succeeded in getting in to

Antigone's tomb in order to die with her only to find
she had already hanged herself. On hearing Haemon's
cry of anguish, Creon entered the tomb too and,
transfixed by the hatred in his son's eyes, endured the
spectacle of Haemon impaling himself on his sword.
Creon's suffering is completed when the Chorus
informs him that in grief at the loss of her son Queen
Eurydice cut her throat. 'You are all alone now,
Creon,' observes the Chorus, who has the last word: 'A
great sad peace descends on Thebes, and on the empty
palace where Creon begins to wait for death.' Yet while
waiting for that death, Creon still has to rule; life has
to go on. He exits with the page to attend a council
meeting called for five o'clock. As the curtain falls, the
last action belongs to the guards, who slam their cards
down on the table and drink their wine. The events of
the day are of little concern to them.

Commentary

Anouilh and the theatre of his time

One of the great formative influences on Anouilh's
early career was seeing Louis Jouvet's production of
Jean Giraudoux's first play *Siegfried* in 1928. He was
only eighteen at the time, and many years later he
described to Paul Vandromme the effect the experience
had on him, 'weeping alone of all the spectators, even
at the funny bits': 'I still know *Siegfried* by heart . . .
That was the night when I suddenly understood.
Thanks to those spring evenings in 1928 I was able to
escape a little from the long night of my existence.'
Historians of twentieth-century French theatre agree
that there are undoubted resemblances between the two
dramatists' themes and techniques (and they are agreed
too on the common debt of both of them to the
sensational discovery of the mid 1920s, the performance
in French translation in Paris of the plays of the Italian
dramatist Luigi Pirandello). At about the same time
Anouilh was also much impressed by the work of Jean
Cocteau, in whose *Eiffel Tower Wedding Party* (*Les
Mariés de la Tour Eiffel*) he claimed to discover a sense
of the 'poetry of the theatre'. This key notion, which is
at the heart of all Cocteau's work in the theatre and is
quite distinct from 'poetic' plays with verse dialogue, is
of importance for an understanding of Anouilh's
theatre. This has been recognised by no less a figure
than Peter Brook: 'Anouilh is a poet, but not a poet of
words: he is a poet of words-acted, of scenes-set, of
players-performing.'

Yet it was only later that this discovery of the 'poetry
of the theatre' made its mark on Anouilh and enabled
him to create the distinctive style of his mature and

enduring plays. His first apprenticeship was in a distinctly naturalistic vein, *L'Hermine* (*The Ermine*, 1931), *Jézabel* (1932) and *La Sauvage* (*The Restless Heart*, 1934), plays in which social and economic factors blight the lives of young lovers, and in some cases drive them to crime and suicide. But an enduring impact of Giraudoux, and to a lesser extent Cocteau, is detectable on Anouilh's work once he begins his run of plays such as *Le Bal des voleurs* (*Thieves' Carnival*, 1932, performed 1938) and *Voyageur sans bagage* (*Traveller without Luggage*, 1937). This latter play is about a man recovering from amnesia who, making a break with his past, has the chance to choose his future. The subject is clearly derived from Giraudoux's *Siegfried*. The plot of Anouilh's play centres on a crucial moment of perception in a person's life, despite which the influence of the past on the present proves to be irrevocable. *Traveller without Luggage* is thematically not so very different from the naturalist style of play that Anouilh was in the process of growing out of, but the treatment is much more structurally assured, sophisticated and 'theatrical'. Above all Anouilh, like Giraudoux, has been marked by the influence of the great Italian master of illusion and manipulator of planes of reality, Pirandello.

The ten years from 1925 to 1935, during which Cocteau, Giraudoux and Pirandello in turn made their mark in Paris before the eyes of the stage-struck young provincial, were ones when a radical change in the aesthetic and moral climate of the French theatre began to have an influence for the better. It was about time. During the second half of the nineteenth century and right up to the First World War (the latter part of that period being the *Belle Époque*), the French theatre was firmly anchored in the mainstream of the entertainment industry catering largely for the affluent *bourgeoisie*. It occupied a slightly superior position in the social scale to music hall and café-concerts – the kind of world in which Anouilh's mother scraped a violin and a living in the provinces. Although currents of avant-garde theatre existed in Paris, the work of those young authors who emerged from it and survived, such as Claudel, Maeterlinck, Courteline and Jarry, was known only to a minority of devotees. The mainstream of theatre-goers, who consumed the vast majority of plays coming off the production line, desired plays that conformed to a realist aesthetic. What was wanted was the kind of neat, ingeniously plotted work along the lines of the 'well-made play' perfected by Eugène Scribe at the beginning of the nineteenth century.

The big names in this tradition – who would all have been well known to Anouilh as a boy – were those of Bernstein, Brieux, Hervieu, Donnay, Porto-Riche, to name just the most successful among hundreds of practitioners. They were adept at supplying an annual flow (usually for an autumn opening) of prosaic, formula-bound plays which would make money for the theatre owners. Some of these writers, as well as their star performers such as Sarah Bernhardt, Mounet-Sully and de Max, the famous 'sacred monsters' of the stage, earned enough money to live legendary existences (Sarah Bernhardt's name is comically dropped by a hack provincial performer in Anouilh's *Eurydice*). The industry also gave employment to an army of lesser actors, theatre professionals and technicians of all sorts, suppliers and contractors. This is not so say that this vein of theatre was invariably mindless entertainment, judged from an artistic and philosophic point of view. It was not unknown for some of these dramatists to address themselves to serious social and moral problems: Eugène Brieux was notably courageous in this respect.

By and large, however, the generation of dramatists that preceded Jean Anouilh were strikingly unimaginative in their whole approach to the available elements of drama: music, décor, mime, lighting and

sound effects, poetry – and, in fact, dialogue in any
form other than mimetic 'real' speech. That
Shakespearean fluidity of time and space that one or
two of their ancestors had attempted to import during
the Romantic period at the beginning of the nineteenth
century had not really taken hold. Theatre design –
insofar as any such clearly delineated profession can be
said to have existed – meant pandering to the
narcissism of the paying customers, dressing star
actresses to their best advantage and making sure the
furniture did not fall over. This is not a skill to be
derided, yet it is one beyond which most professional
French theatre people did not aspire to progress at a
time when the artistic basis of theatre was being
radically transformed outside France by the designs and
theories of such important pioneers as Adolphe Appia
and Edward Gordon Craig.

Fortunately, this state of affairs did not go
unchallenged in the years preceding the First World
War. The artistic and literary objections to the
commercial mainstream of French theatre at this time –
which in its provincial touring form will be satirised by
Anouilh in *Eurydice* – were expressed with force by a
small number of intellectuals. In a lecture in Brussels in
1904, André Gide, who was to become one of France's
leading novelists, delivered a powerful critique of the
contemporary French theatre: the success of a theatrical
venture, he argued, was related to just about every
factor other than the literary or artistic merits of the
play itself. In fact any dramatist who was ambitious
artistically was putting his chances of being performed
in serious jeopardy. In 1913 the actor and director
Jacques Copeau continued the campaign in an article
published in the *Nouvelle Revue Française* entitled 'Un
Essai de rénovation dramatique'. His denunciation was
even more vehement and comprehensive in its range of
targets than Gide's: dramatists, performers, theatre
critics, above all the 'shameless merchants' who owned

theatres and financed productions to make money. The
puritanical tone of the article is typical of the man.
Copeau was a dedicated theorist and director who is
credited with having started the long march to a
French theatre of the highest artistic standards in
opening his Théâtre du Vieux Colombier in the Paris
Latin Quarter in the same year.

So Jean Anouilh was born at exactly the right time,
1910. By the late 1920s, having moved as a schoolboy
to Paris from his birthplace, Bordeaux, the French
theatre was ready for him. The professional
environment had been transformed, thanks to the
efforts of Copeau and the generation of directors who
followed in his wake, Georges Pitoëff, Charles Dullin,
Gaston Baty and Louis Jouvet. As an ambitious young
man determined to make his living solely from writing
for the theatre, Anouilh was soon welcomed by a
profession and a theatre-going public that left little to
be desired. This was a theatre world that was at last
receptive to imaginative revivals of the French classics
and the masterpieces of the world repertory – hence the
many successful productions of Musset, Shakespeare,
Calderón, Ibsen, Chekhov, Shaw and Pirandello in the
1920s and 30s. And it was just as receptive to new
French authors who might fulfil Copeau's aim of re-
creating for the French theatre 'its lustre and its
grandeur'. By the mid 1930s Claudel, Cocteau,
Giraudoux and Salacrou were contributing to the
achievement of that aim, and Anouilh would soon be
ready to join their ranks. Once he had learnt the basics
of his craft by completing his apprenticeship in the
school of naturalism, he set about developing a more
personal style. The performances of *Traveller without
Luggage* (1937) and *Thieves' Carnival* (1938) were a
turning point; Anouilh's artistic signature was confident
and legible. In these and the plays that followed he had
the technical skill to handle intricate plot structures and
time sequences, and plunge his audiences into a clearly

unnaturalistic exploration of planes of illusion and 'reality'. Above all, his at times exuberant and ostentatious theatricality was to be put at the service of wide-ranging historic, legendary and mythic themes.

Antigone is one of four plays Anouilh derived from ancient Greek mythic themes, the others being *Eurydice*, *Médée* and *Tu étais si gentil quand tu étais petit* (You Used To Be Such a Nice Little Boy; based on the *Oresteia* family cycle). These 'Greek' plays may be assimilated to a larger number of plays by Anouilh on legendary or historical subjects, as they operate in a very similar way dramatically: *L'Alouette* (*The Lark*; Joan of Arc), *Ornifle* (Don Juan), *Pauvre Bitos ou le dîner de têtes* (*Poor Bitos*; Robespierre and other leaders of the French Revolution), *Becket ou l'honneur de Dieu* (Thomas à Becket and Henry II), *La Foire d'empoigne* (Catch as Catch Can; Napoleon and Louis XVIII). In some of Anouilh's programme notes (virtually the only source of personal statements about his work) he has been remarkably frank – and provocative – in denying any concern for the truth of history:

> '*La Foire d'empoigne* is a farce in which of course any resemblance to the real Napoleon and Louis XVIII is purely accidental.'

> '. . . this weary, undernourished, haggard young girl (yes, I know she was a strapping lass, but I don't care) and strangely obstinate . . . Joan of Arc cannot be explained.'

> 'I just hope the English will forgive me for this play – and for some standard jokes which I can never get out of my system. I didn't go looking in history books for the real Henry II – nor even Becket. I created the type of King I needed and the ambivalent Becket I needed.'

Anouilh thus admitted making use of historical subject matter to provide himself with the type of character *he needed*. And so it is with other sources of plot. Whether he is using the cloudiest of myths such as that of

Orpheus and Eurydice, or relatively verifiable modern
history (Robespierre and Napoleon I), Anouilh is
looking for *pre*texts [*sic*], for basic scenarios to
assimilate to his own private universe. These scenarios
are often structured on diametrically opposed human
types or legendary conflicts, such as the
Antigone–Creon and Don Juan–Sganarelle antitheses,
which have been exploited many times before in the
theatre. Others may be distortions of history or even
complete fabrications by the author to suit his purpose,
as is the case in *Becket, Poor Bitos* and *La Foire
d'empoigne*.

Let us now look at this private universe to which
Anouilh assimilates all myth, all history. It has to be
admitted that although he soon left behind the
naturalistic *manner* of crafting plays, the mood did not
change. The bleak moral and human climate of those
early works stayed with Anouilh throughout most of his
mature career. A profoundly despairing vision of the
world is presented in the majority of Anouilh's plays,
and it is significant that roughly half of those written in
the period surrounding *Antigone* are grouped in volumes
entitled 'Black Plays' (see note on categories of
Anouilh's plays p. v–vi). In fact all four of Anouilh's
Greek plays are in some measure situated in the
emotionally damaged core of a dysfunctional family.
The boy who 'used-to-be-so-nice' is the unfortunate
Orestes, son of Agamemnon and Clytemnestra, who are
possibly the most propitiously sinister of all parents in
literary history for Anouilh's lifelong theme. The plays
written around the time of *Antigone* and *Eurydice* are
totally centred on heroes and heroines who struggle to
preserve their integrity in a world which is mean, ugly
and corrupt. This integrity may mean purity in an
orthodox moral sense, but it often also means freedom
as an unhampered personality. In one strikingly
Freudian example, *Medea*, integrity even has the
biological force of the word with which it is

etymologically linked, *entirety*. The tragic heroine
Medea bitterly regrets that she is a woman; she feels
'amputated' sexually, thus castrated, not 'entire' (she
actually uses the equivalent French adjective) in the
technical sense used by veterinary surgeons in both
French and English. This is not a lurid footnote, for we
shall see that Antigone too will resent not being male.

In most cases the heroes and heroines are young, in
early adulthood, coming into a painful confrontation
with the values of their parents, the 'realists' who
survive by means of guile and compromise, and the
abandonment of any idealism that they may once have
possessed. Love, like human beauty, is transient: it is
neither eternal nor unique. It is defeated, as the
General says in *Ardèle*, by life. The only attainable
absolute is death. Play after play builds up to the
moment of confrontation, the point at which the
protagonist chooses to cry 'No!', to reject the offer of
integration into the world of mitigated contentment
inhabited by most human beings. Even in the 'Pink
Plays', where a more light-hearted tone prevails,
Anouilh tends to pattern his characterisation on the
same Romantic antitheses. Where he parts company
with the Romantics, however, is in denying his
characters all hope of a spiritual or ideological refuge.
The rebel son or daughter rejecting the parents' world
of bourgeois hypocrisy is seldom tempted by the idea
that might have been entertained in Romantic drama,
namely that salvation lies in poverty and the simple life.
Poverty in Anouilh corrupts every bit as much as
wealth; it humiliates and brutalises its victims and scars
them for life. Other misfortunes are equally
irremediable: a joyless childhood, physical ugliness and
a traumatic initiation to sexuality. Nor are these
youthful rebels interested in striving for a society in
which the young will not be scarred by poverty, or
women (and, for that matter, men) sexually humiliated:
not for nothing is a study by A.F. Rombout of the

quest for purity in Anouilh's moral universe subtitled
'l'anarchisme réactionnaire'. Political commitment on
progressive lines is either absent from Anouilh's theatre,
or, when it makes a marginal appearance in a few of
the later plays, cruelly parodied in the form of
grotesque feminists or trade unionists. The vast
majority of Anouilh's characters exist in a unique moral
and social vacuum. It is a vision of man as an
irredeemably egocentric creature, a vision which
Anouilh claimed to discern in the French dramatist
whom he admired most of all, the seventeenth-century
classicist, Molière, 'author of civilised comedies which
are the blackest theatre of all time' (quoted by
P. Vandromme, *Jean Anouilh, un auteur et ses
personnages* – see Further Reading, p. lvi for details of
all references).

Greek myth in twentieth-century French theatre

During the great revival of the French theatre in the
middle of the twentieth century, Anouilh was not the
only dramatist who, exploring myth, history and legend
as a vehicle for modern moral and philosophical
dilemmas, found that Greek myth was especially fertile.
More of his contemporaries than is realised either made
original plays out of Greek myths or adapted the extant
plays of the three great tragedians, Aeschylus,
Sophocles and Euripides. They were thus following an
illustrious precedent in French theatre history for
writing new versions of the tragedies of classical
antiquity, particularly those of Euripides. Three
centuries before the surge of Greek-inspired plays by
Cocteau, Giraudoux, Sartre, Anouilh and others,
Corneille's *Médée* was performed in 1635. This was a
version of Euripides' *Medea*, and it was the same Greek
tragedian's work which inspired three of Racine's
masterpieces later in the century: *Andromaque* (1667),
Iphigénie (1674) and *Phèdre* (1677). He also wrote *La*

Thébaïde (1664), which is derived from the Theban cycle mostly associated with Sophocles and the source of Anouilh's *Antigone* too. Dramatic writing based on Greek myth, inspired by Renaissance scholarship, did not peak again in neo-classical France and in fact faltered during the eighteenth century. In the early decades of the next century the proponents of the Romantic movement considered it one of their most important principles to shun classical inspiration, in part because it was associated with pre-Revolutionary France. Thus the major part of the plays of dramatists such as Victor Hugo, the elder Alexandre Dumas and Alfred de Musset were based on mediaeval and Renaissance European themes, or contemporary life.

During the second half of the nineteenth century, thanks to the considerable advances made in classical scholarship and the beginnings of modern archaeology, a renewed interest was taken in ancient drama and the way in which it was performed. In the excavated Roman amphitheatre at Orange in the South of France open-air drama festivals were held, during which the plays of antiquity, Roman as well as Greek, were put on as authentically as current knowledge permitted. Yet no French dramatists of any stature felt the desire to write serious plays on Greek mythic themes at this time. It may seem curious perhaps that just when a far better understanding of ancient theatre was developing in the nineteenth century, the only original dramatic exploitations were Offenbach's comic operas *Orphée aux enfers* (*Orpheus in the Underworld*, 1858, libretto by Crémieux and Halévy) and *La Belle Hélène* (1864, libretto and original play by Meilhac and Halévy). In these works the ancient myths were vigorously debunked via a stream of facetious anachronisms and, more importantly perhaps, they served as a vehicle for a satirical attack on the less heroic world of French bourgeois and upper-class society in the Second Empire period.

It need not be a surprise that this kind of Greek-derived operetta flourished in Paris at the same time as authentic and reverential productions of the original tragedies were being put on in places like Orange. And for the purposes of this survey the coincidence of the two modes prepares us for what followed in heralding the spirit of much twentieth-century theatre. From the 1920s French theatre was quite hospitable to a juxtaposition, or even fusion, of seemingly disparate tones, the solemn and the satirical, the elegiac and the ironic; indeed many would argue that the greatest French theatre of the century is in essence definable in terms of this dual tonality. The ironic mode is never repressed for long, for example, in the work of Giraudoux, Cocteau and Sartre, who all recycled the most awesome of Greek tragedies at least once as a vehicle for comment on twentieth-century society. The phenomenon was widespread; the following list is just a selection of the better known plays:

Paul Claudel	*Protée*, 1913 (*Proteus*)
Jean Cocteau	*Antigone*, 1922 (a translation/'contraction')
	Orphée, 1926 (*Orpheus*)
	La Machine infernale, 1934 (*The Infernal Machine*)
André Gide	*Oedipe*, 1930 (*Oedipus*)
Jean Giraudoux	*Amphitryon 38*, 1929 (allegedly the thirty-eighth play on an Amphitryon theme)
	La Guerre de Troie n'aura pas lieu, 1935 (The Trojan War Will Not Take Place, translated by Christopher Fry as *Tiger at the Gates*)
	Electre, 1937 (*Electra*)
Jean Anouilh	*Eurydice*, 1941
	Antigone, 1944
	Médée, 1946 (performed 1953)
	Tu étais si gentil quand tu étais petit, 1972

Jean-Paul Sartre	*Les Mouches*, 1942 (*The Flies*)
Henri Ghéon	*Oedipe*, 1942
Georges Neveux	*Le Voyage de Thésée*, 1943 (Theseus's Journey)
'Mme Simone' (Pauline Porché)	*Descente aux enfers*, 1947 (Descent into Hell)
Robert Merle	*Sisyphe et la mort*, 1950 (Sisyphus and Death)
André Obey	*Une fille pour du vent*, 1953 (A Fair Wind for Iphigenia)

The titles of a few of these plays are ironic in themselves. Giraudoux, for example, would have enjoyed the thought that some scholar on the surface of the planet would be counting the number of plays known to have been written on the Amphitryon theme only to end up very puzzled. Others give no clue as to the genre. Paul Claudel's *Protée* is a spirited pastiche of a satyr-play (the type of comic-relief conclusion to a Greek trilogy of tragedies), in which the spectator enjoys the discomfort of Menelaus when he is stranded on Naxos with the mindless Helen of Troy. In similar vein, Robert Merle's *Sisyphe et la mort* is a joke at the expense of the eminently provokable Albert Camus, whose rather obscure mythic figure Sisyphus had been presented as a philosophic hero of our time in the much acclaimed *Mythe de Sisyphe* in 1942. Other plays are not in the least comic and contain no leavening of irony or parody. This is the case with Anouilh's *Medea*, which is not so very different from its model, Euripides' tragedy about a vengeful deserted wife. In Mme Simone's play about the German Occupation, the *maquisard* hero Alcestis raids a Hades resembling a kind of labour camp ruled by SS officers. It is a grim subject grimly handled, and it must be said that by 1947 the author is making a late jump on to a bandwagon that has run its course and is no longer hailed with enthusiasm by critics and reviewers.

How does one explain this modern French resurgence of interest in Greek myth? Amiably parodic works such as Merle's *Sisyphe et la mort* need no accounting for, as parasitic sketches have always fed off successful literary movements in France. One of the very first 'neo-Greek' plays, Cocteau's *Orphée*, was partly that kind of dramatic joke itself, a satire on Surrealist and Dadaist pretension in the early 1920s (as well as being a genuine personal statement by the author about the poet's vocation). It is easy to account for imitators, but what caused the surge of interest in Greek myth in the creative imagination of dramatists like Cocteau and Giraudoux in the first place? The beginnings of an answer can be found early in the century, 1923, but neither in theatre nor in fact in French literature. In a review entitled '*Ulysses,* order and myth' (in *The Dial,* November 1923), T.S. Eliot had this to say about James Joyce's masterpiece:

> In using the myth, in manipulating a continuous parallel between contemporaneity and antiquity, Mr Joyce is pursuing a method which others must pursue after him. They will not be imitators, any more than the scientist who uses the discoveries of Einstein in pursuing his own, independent, further investigations. It is simply a way of controlling, or ordering, of giving a shape and significance to the immense panorama of futility and anarchy which is contemporary history.

Much later than T.S. Eliot, after the neo-Greek movement in the French theatre had declined and could be seen in perspective, academic critics took up again this question of its philosophical significance. Jacqueline Duchemin was thus expressing very 1960s sentiments when she argued that the widespread recourse to Greek archetypal myths can best be interpreted in the light of the theories of the great Swiss psychiatrist-psychologist Carl Gustav Jung. That is to say that the fundamental human dilemmas which are at the heart of the myths corresponded in some measure with the preoccupations weighing on the French *collective unconscious* (the Jungian term) at this time. The body of ancient Greek analogies, with which an educated French public would be more familiar than any other in Europe, served as a framework of reassurance in an age of crisis and doubt. Duchemin went so far as to make the surprising claim that in certain fundamental respects – those affecting an individual's place in the universe and even the destiny of mankind itself – modern French dramatists may have been closer in spirit to the earlier of the Greek tragedians, Aeschylus and Sophocles, than were their seventeenth-century predecessors. Racine and his contemporaries were attracted mostly to the last of the ancient trio, Euripides, whose universe was more individual-based and humanistic, less cosmic and polytheistic than that of Aeschylus and Sophocles. No one was more skilled than Racine in the seventeenth century at exploiting what is at the heart of certain of Euripides' tragedies: all-consuming passion both emotionally and physically. Racine elaborated this into a thoroughly ambiguous phenomenon, an irrevocable love entanglement that is both exquisitely thrilling and devastatingly destructive for all concerned. Whoever experienced it lived on a moral knife-edge – and often died on a real one. In this way did Racine entertain the sophisticated court élite of Louis XIV (J. Duchemin, 'Les survivances des mythes antiques dans le théâtre français', *Bulletin de l'Association Guillaume Budé*, Paris, 1964, p.93). Of course, the love relationship at the heart of Aeschylus's *Oresteia* and Sophocles' *King Oedipus* is also devastating in its consequences, but devastating for the whole of Troy, Argos and Thebes, exactly as the gods had warned. For Euripides, drawing on the same corpus of myths, the scale of things is different: a delinquent lover's innards seared by a deadly potion burn as fiercely as the whole of Troy.

In a discussion following the lecture that was the basis of Duchemin's article, Defradas concurred, observing that in 1634 Corneille too found what he wanted in Euripides. He took up his *Medea* because its core of sexual jealousy and revenge made for an eventful plot, and it would be possible to keep that plot bowling along by recycling the tragic heroine as a seventeenth-century baroque sorceress with a magic ring. Conversely, Defradas argued, what was profoundly metaphysical in the ancient myths was either so morally and aesthetically repugnant to the sensibility of Corneille's and Racine's contemporaries, or so beyond their understanding, that it was transformed almost beyond recognition or avoided altogether. His conclusion was that 'a true knowledge of Greek myth has been reborn in our time and in the work of our modern authors' (my translation, see Defradas in *Bulletin* above, p.103).

So it has been argued persuasively by recent scholars that in appropriating the myths of ancient Greece to explore modern crises and dilemmas, dramatists like Cocteau, Giraudoux, Sartre and Anouilh, among many others, have understood and recaptured the spirit of those myths better than did their seventeenth-century predecessors. Let us now look at *Antigone* in the light of this claim, which may be surprising to many. On the face of it, 'futility and anarchy', the terms used by T.S. Eliot to link ancient and modern contexts, would seem to be particularly apt words to bear in mind when considering the rebellion in the soul of Anouilh's heroine. Let us first see what might have attracted him in Sophocles' *Antigone*; it is undoubtedly Anouilh's source, and it is as well we should know certain things about it.

Sophocles and the myth of Antigone

As is the case with Aeschylus and Euripides, only a very small part of Sophocles' dramatic output has

survived. *Antigone*, which was performed in 441 BC, is
one of the most admired of his seven extant tragedies,
and one of the three plays making up the Theban
Cycle. They relate to each other in the chronological
order *King Oedipus, Oedipus at Colonus, Antigone* as
regards the events making up their plots, although that
is not the order in which they were written. *Antigone*
was written a long time before the first two, and there
are slight inconsistencies in the plots of the plays. They
are thus not a trilogy in the precise sense of three
coherently related plays all written and performed at
the same time.

   In *Antigone* Sophocles deals with the continuing
aftermath of the havoc caused in the first part of the
cycle by Oedipus's arrogance in thinking it possible to
disregard a prediction by the Oracle of Apollo that he
would kill his father and marry his mother. His parents
Laius and Jocasta had previously sought to defy the
prediction by leaving him to perish as an infant, but
they did not know that he had survived. Oedipus was
brought up by Polybus king of Corinth and his wife
Merope, believing them to be his real parents.
However, both parts of the awesome prediction were
eventually fulfilled: Oedipus did kill his father and
marry his mother but did so not knowing who they
were. On his way to Thebes, he killed an old man in a
quarrel at a crossroads (the first 'road rage' crime in
literary history) and when he arrived he married the
widowed Jocasta. Although he acted in ignorance –
believing himself safe once Polybus and Merope were
dead – that was no excuse in the eyes of Sophocles'
audiences of the fifth century BC. Oedipus brought
down upon himself and his clan a terrible retribution
from the gods. Jocasta took her life on discovering the
identity of her youthful second husband, by whom she
had had two sons, Eteocles and Polynices, and two
daughters, Ismene and Antigone. Oedipus blinded

himself in remorse, having also realised who the old
man was whom he had killed at the crossroads.
Accompanied only by Antigone, Oedipus left Thebes
and died in exile, having been given sanctuary at
Colonus by King Theseus of Athens.

The curse on the house continued. Eteocles and
Polynices were meant to alternate as rulers of Thebes,
but fought a savage civil war for sole control of the
city. Both died in it in single combat and Jocasta's
brother Creon became king. As Eteocles had been king
at the time of the conflict with his brother, he was
given a state funeral; the body of Polynices, however,
was to be left to rot, unburied, as a warning to future
would-be traitors. Creon further ordered that death
would be the fate of anyone attempting to bury the
body. All of this is the material of the first two plays in
Sophocles' cycle; his *Antigone* begins a very short while
after the death of the brothers and the end of the civil
war, just as does Anouilh's version.

The most important point to be born in mind when
it comes to comparing the two plays is that in
Sophocles' version Creon is very much the central
figure. Although Antigone is locked in conflict with him
because she is adamant about doing what is morally
paramount, burying her brother, she is absent from the
last quarter of the play once she has been sent to her
death. From that point on, Creon is the sole tragic
focus. He is left to pay a terrible price for his 'tyranny'
by realising that he has also caused the suicide of his
son Haemon, who is betrothed to Antigone, and in
turn of his wife Eurydice. Although he needed to
restore order to Thebes, Creon is deemed by everyone
in the play to be wrong, both sacrilegious and a tyrant,
in denying funeral rites to a dead man, however
traitorous. Moral outrage at Creon's intransigence is
expressed most powerfully by the blind prophet
Tiresias. Creon is alarmed by the latter's dire warnings,
and at last he yields – but it is too late. He thus

experiences a realisation of the truth, *anagnorisis*:
through his pride he has 'unwittingly' killed his son and
his wife (there is no thought now for Antigone). With
the two bodies in front of him, Creon is a chastened
and stricken man at the end of the play, with nothing
but the solemn moralising of the Chorus for comfort.

Although Antigone would thus appear to be of
secondary importance to Creon in the Sophocles
version, it is the heroine who has grown in the
imagination of dramatists and philosophers from the
Renaissance onwards who have been inspired by his
play. From Garnier's *Antigone ou la Piété* (1580) to
Brecht's *Antigone* (1947), the devoted daughter of
Oedipus and principled sister of Polynices, virgin and
willing martyr, has been recruited, often heavily
disguised, to stiffen the sinews of those fighting many
causes. A Christian martyr, a Joan of Arc figure, a
fervent egalitarian in the French Revolution, a daughter
of Louis XVI, victim of that revolution, a Republican
resisting the Prussians in 1870, a privileged German
waking up too late to the menace of Nazism, all of
these 'avatars' of Antigone and more are discussed by
Simone Fraisse in *Le Mythe d'Antigone*. Furthermore,
her myth has evolved. Fraisse concludes that in the last
two centuries, consistently with changes in modern
society, Antigone's religious and family importance has
decreased at the same time as her political stature has
grown. She appeals to the imagination increasingly,
Fraisse argues, as a political heroine, the enemy of all
tyranny: 'for the French in particular Antigone will
always be the daughter of the Revolution.'

Anouilh's *Antigone*

Of all modern French plays derived from ancient Greek
tragedies, *Antigone* is by far the closest to its source as
regards the basic plot. Yet the changes that Anouilh
does make, although in some cases seemingly slight,

suffice to make it a very different work both as a
theatrical experience and as a play charged with moral
and political meaning.

The first and most striking difference is an artistic
one. From the moment the curtain goes up, a member
of the Chorus steps forward to act as Prologue,
'presenting' the whole plot and cast of the play –
'Twelve Characters in Search of a Tragedy', as it were.
Antigone is thus located in theatre history as very much
the kind of French play that followed in the wake of
Pirandello in the 1930s and 40s. The function of the
Prologue-Chorus is quite different from that of his
ancestor in Sophocles and of great importance in this
play (the role is so substantial that in the London Old
Vic production of 1949 it was the one that Laurence
Olivier played rather than that of Creon). The
Prologue-Chorus is a member of the cast, a performer,
and yet he detaches himself from the play at various
times to address the audience, stressing the theatricality
of what it is witnessing. In a key speech he makes a
serious artistic and philosophical distinction between
melodrama, in which the plot depends upon chance
(and the heroine is usually saved on the cliff edge), and
tragedy, where the outcome is known in advance and
unavoidable; the latter is what he, and through him
Anouilh, clearly believes *Antigone* to be.

A play in which there are constant direct and indirect
reminders that what we are watching is a play is
considered in modern critical parlance to be
'metatheatre'. Anouilh is very good at this, and for
many critics it is his artistic trademark. He creates a
similar ('metatheatrical', or 'self-referential') effect in a
number of other plays, although without again using a
Prologue-Chorus, i.e. a compère, master of ceremonies.
Needless to say, this sophisticated type of formal
distancing is quite absent from Sophocles and all other
classical tragedy. This is not at all to say that the latter
is artistically primitive; it is sophisticated in other ways,

for example by means of elements absent from Anouilh:
dance, choric recitation, and variations in dialogue
style, verse and metre.

There is another side to this metatheatrical element
in Anouilh's *Antigone*, however. Students of the play
must ask themselves whether this ironic distancing –
and particularly the inserted lesson about the
unavoidability of the heroine's fate – does not in fact
reduce, or even totally destroy, its tragic impact. Walter
Ince ('Prologue and Chorus in Anouilh's *Antigone*', in
Forum for Modern Language Studies, IV, pp.277-84)
claims that the lesson 'causes us to think too much and
especially to become aware of the great difference
between classical tragedy and metatheatre'. In other
words, Ince argues, Anouilh cannot have it both ways,
metatheatre and tragedy. He is worth quoting further:

> [The lesson] can also provoke in us the reflection that the
> Chorus' description of tragedy is incomplete, for although
> it is convincing to stress its inevitability, Anouilh omits the
> transcendental element which underlies the traditional
> tragic figure. The sweeping nature of his theme of 'sale
> espoir' ['lousy hope'] is surely inimical to tragedy. If life
> evokes such complete hopelessness, where is the tragedy in
> leaving it? In disaster or in struggle, tragedy implies the
> affirmation of some value or values and has to that extent
> never been utterly pessimistic (if only for the audience as
> distinct from the characters in the play). In Sophocles'
> version, Haemon and Antigone do not seek death but the
> fact that they are willing to die for their beliefs asserts the
> value of family piety and individual liberty against the
> tyrannical Creon, who is punished by his sufferings.
>
> (p.282)

Ince's argument is a powerful one, and only slightly
weakened by the fact that he does not appear to have
noticed (and he can hardly be blamed) something
about Antigone's final moments that we shall discuss
later: when she is about to die Antigone admits, but to

herself alone, that she is in the wrong – she could and
should have agreed to live. In all its imperfection life is
still worth living. That is the 'affirmation of value' quite
rightly looked for in tragedy by Ince that Anouilh could
have made more than just a fleeting realisation by
Antigone.

That Antigone evolves only so partially and
ambivalently at the end relates to another change that
is evident from the play's earliest moments. Anouilh
has created the character of the nurse, an old palace
retainer to whom the heroine is very close. For some
critics the sentimentality of her scenes with Antigone is
cloying and as such an artistic blemish. But regardless
of that issue of taste and tone, the invention of the role
makes it clear that a major philosophical theme of the
play, as indeed of many others by Anouilh, is *childhood*.
There are numerous reminders: for example, it is with
a child's seaside spade that she covers her brother's
body. Antigone was an untameable, tomboyish child,
yet dreamy, a child of nature. Now she is thin and
underdeveloped as a woman like other Anouilh
heroines, and she has no more begun to mature
emotionally than she has physically. Antigone will not
be the last of Anouilh's heroines for whom the trauma
of leaving behind the innocence and security of
childhood is too much to bear. The point is further
emphasised by Creon in the very last moments of the
play when he tells the young pageboy that he is 'mad'
to be looking forward to growing up: 'It would be best
never to grow up.'

Creon thus understands what Antigone has gone
through, and appears to sympathise with her. He saw
that her determination to bury Polynices was 'only an
excuse' (Ismene had also objected that he was a
brother who had never shown any kindness to his
sisters). Antigone's insistence on burying her brother is
thus a way of contriving an end to her life – 'she
wanted to die', in Creon's words. This is very different

from Sophocles' Antigone, who feels compelled to bury
her brother because of

> . . . ancient moralities
> Or common human decency.
> They speak the language of eternity,
> Are not written down, and never change.
> They are for today, yesterday, and all time.
> No one understands where they came from,
> But everyone recognises their force:
> And no man's arrogance or power
> Can make me disobey them.
>
> (*Antigone* in *Sophocles Plays: One*, translated by Don
> Taylor, p. 151)

There is never any shadow of a doubt that this is her
true motivation, and her courageous observance of this
duty and vigorous defence of the principle before
Creon would have been totally approved of by the
Athenian audience. That Creon is wrong and Antigone
right is argued most forcefully of all by the blind
prophet Tiresias, whose moral authority and fiery
imprecations are sufficient to make Creon repent of his
decision. It is no coincidence that Tiresias is the one
character completely omitted from Anouilh's play: the
religious dimension is not apt and in fact Creon speaks
contemptuously of the priests who officiate at funerals
as clock-watching functionaries racing shamelessly
through the ritual to finish in time for lunch. In
Anouilh's lay universe, which very much has a
twentieth-century feel to it, Antigone's brief fears about
her brother's unburied spirit wandering eternally are
unconvincing in a context of night-clubs, fast cars and
gambling debts; it would have been better to omit them
altogether.

Another modification of the original source brings
Antigone firmly within Anouilh's private orbit: the
lengthy scene he has invented between Antigone and
Haemon. In Sophocles' play they are accepted as
betrothed and that is it. A love relationship as

extensively *portrayed* as it is in Anouilh would have
been quite foreign to Sophocles and his audiences –
and a timid offer by the princess of premarital sex,
abhorrent. But the difference is more fundamental than
that. In Anouilh it is not a case of the filling out of a
romantic relationship in the modern European tradition,
so that we might appreciate the strength of the girl's
sacrifice. Rather, Antigone forfeits her life because
among the nightmarish prospects that lie ahead in adult
life is that of Haemon ceasing to be 'demanding and
loyal', becoming 'just a conventional spouse and
learning to say yes like the rest'. And in Anouilh's
universe the adjective 'ugly' (*laid*), although still used
primarily as a term of moral condemnation, never
completely loses its physical resonance: we are right to
suspect that Antigone also fears the day when her
future husband will inherit his father's corpulence and
care-lined face.

And so to that father, uncle and 'tyrant', Creon.
Here the change is quite radical. Whereas Sophocles'
king of Thebes was odious in a number of respects,
autocratic, ill-tempered, and contemptuous of women,
Anouilh's is human and sensitive, loath to tell Antigone
the cruel truth about her brothers, only to be reviled by
her for making every attempt to save her from what
amounts to suicide. Another important difference is
that Anouilh also means us to see him as justified
politically in issuing such a harsh edict: desperate times
require desperate measures (and we shall have more to
say about this). The transformation of the character is
so great that Anouilh relieves him of the burden of
culpability at the end of the play. Creon is stricken at
the death of his son and wife, but cannot be held
responsible for these catastrophes; he can only be pitied
for his personal loss. Creon's character is then further
enhanced by his fortitude in carrying straight on the
same day with the thankless task of governing Thebes.

In Anouilh it is Antigone, not Creon, who

experiences an emergence from darkness into the light,
something like a moment of *anagnorisis*, in realising
when it is too late that she has been wrong. She
confesses to the guard that she no longer knows what
she is dying for, and that she could and should have
agreed to live: 'It's only now I realise how easy it was
to live . . .' But then, in a disturbing moment of
inconsistency and perhaps even cowardice that no
commentator has picked up, she prevents that truth
from being known, making the guard delete the
confession from the letter she is dictating to Haemon.
So Anouilh's tortured idealist thirsting for a world of
purity and eternal innocence, the fiery adolescent who
until now has execrated the subterfuges and lies of the
world of adults such as Creon, perpetrates a sin of
omission, a kind of lie, of her own: 'It's better no one
should ever know.' She thus dies in a state of confusion
and self-deceit. The French term for the latter is
mauvaise foi; it is not ever any part of Anouilh's
vocabulary, but the phenomenon can be found in his
work. Contemporaries such as Jean-Paul Sartre in the
period of committed literature of the 1940s and 50s,
however, were fascinated by it as a literary motif, and it
could be argued that Antigone dies as confused and
ambivalent as Sartre's equally enigmatic hero Hugo
Barine in *Les Mains sales* (*Crime Passionnel*, 1948).
Antigone's last moments of life are thus shot through
with philosophic irony, but it is an effect that we
cannot be certain that Anouilh intended. At all events,
morally his *Antigone* is a very different play from
Sophocles'.

Finally, as a theatrical experience too, the play is very
different. The most obvious way is the one that meets
the eye first as the characters are waiting to be
introduced: modern dress and a neutral, non-Greek
décor. Modern dress in February 1944 in the first
French production meant dress suits and white tie for
the upper-class men, black leather coats for the guards,

long black gowns for the women, with Ismene alone in
white. In productions since then the same principle of
elegant but sober neutrality has generally been kept to.
Then we notice that some of the characters are knitting
or playing cards: the tone is very different too. While
lighter moments are not totally absent from Sophocles'
play – the long-winded guard severely tests Creon's
patience – Anouilh is much more systematic in varying
the range of moods and tones in his *Antigone*. He
considerably expands the role of Sophocles' guard and
gives him two colleagues for good measure. Between
them they occupy the stage a not insignificant amount
of time and they also have a moral and philosophic role
that Sophocles' guard does not. Socially speaking, they
could be the brothers or sons of the nurse, at the
opposite end of the scale from Creon and Antigone. In
their intellectual and moral mediocrity, their vulgarity
of speech and insensitivity in front of Antigone, they
exemplify Anouilh's lack of illusions about the common
man. They are a source of low comedy and black
humour, but must be seen as providing far more than
just 'comic relief'. That it is the leading guard, a man
hopelessly lacking in dignity and human warmth, who
is chosen by the dramatist as Antigone's last contact –
and is anyone surprised that when questioned by her he
turns out to be an average married man with two
children? – is one of the best indicators of *Antigone*'s
'Black Plays' category. As if that is not enough, it is the
indifference and callousness of all three guards which
Anouilh selects as a moral spectacle on which to bring
down the curtain, in preference to the brief moral
conclusion of Sophocles' Chorus.

Critics have thus sometimes taxed Anouilh with
misanthropy for his portrait of the guards and through
them the human race in such a way as to justify
Creon's cynicism. Some can detect in him too a
measure of misogyny for his creation of a wittering,
unintelligent nurse and, conversely, for his reduction of

the dignified Eurydice we find in Sophocles to a non-speaking role, a twee *Homes and Gardens* matriarch. Perhaps the anachronisms are indeed a miscalculation this time, a 'glaring lapse of taste' in the words of W.D. Howarth (*Anouilh: Antigone*). These question-marks over the tastefulness or otherwise of Anouilh's modernising features, including the racy, idiomatic speech of some of the characters, will always be a critical grey area, inviting a personal response from students of this controversial play. There need be no orthodoxy on an artistic aspect of twentieth-century theatre where such highly individual dramatists as Cocteau, Giraudoux and Sartre walked the same tightrope.

What has never been anything other than admired, however, is the skill that has gone into Anouilh's finest innovation (the word is not too strong), the climactic confrontation between Creon and Antigone. This takes up one third of the play and is thus many times longer than the equivalent scene in Sophocles. It is morally and psychologically more complex; it is far less diluted, furthermore, in its emotional tension and power than that scene is in Sophocles by Ismene's entrance to announce her change of heart. Anouilh's scene is a masterpiece of dramatic construction, as he leads us gradually to the realisation that far from being a brutal tyrant Creon has a plausible case for acting as he has done. Conversely, the same skilful technique leads us also to the realisation that Antigone's ostensibly noble cause is insincere, an excuse by an emotionally unstable young person to spare herself the looming disappointments of adult life.

The scene builds up to two successive peaks. The first is the moment when, having failed completely to win from Antigone any understanding of his political plight, Creon throws the last card in his hand in desperation. His twin revelations about the character of her brothers and the impossibility of identifying the

mangled corpses is doubly crushing, and it succeeds as
a way of getting her to back down. Or nearly. After
more than twenty minutes of the greatest suspense -
having been skilfully hooked by Anouilh and pulled this
way and that by the antagonists' competing appeals to
feeling and intelligence – the audience's relief is short-
lived. Out of the most understandable of human
motives, Creon makes the fatal mistake of
recommending orthodox *happiness* to Antigone. That
word is enough to spark a rebellion that is this time
irrepressible. The scene rises to a new peak of tension,
culminating in insults, turmoil and the physical removal
of Antigone.

Students of this play, then, are invited to admire this
famous scene in particular, a classic conflict in a
modern context, constructed by a virtuoso of mid-
twentieth-century theatricality. They should be made
aware too that, particularly in France, the scene has
been much discussed for other reasons. Anouilh has
been criticised for transforming Sophocles' mature,
lucid and heroic young woman who dies for a principle
into a hysterical adolescent who dies for nothing,
defeated by the confirmation that mankind is imperfect
and life is difficult. More controversial still is Anouilh's
portrait of a twentieth-century Creon.

Antigone in performance: the 1944 controversy and after

'Antigone is right – but Creon is not wrong': this was
how Albert Camus summed up the core conflict that
he considered to lie at the heart of all tragedy. He was
speaking in 1955 in a lecture on the Future of Tragedy,
delivered in Athens, and went on in that essay to make
the same distinctions as Anouilh's Prologue-Chorus
between melodrama and tragedy. Camus appears to
have had in mind the modern *Antigone* in that he
focused on an aspect of the myth that preoccupied

Anouilh rather more than it did the ancient tragedian,
creating an equilibrium between the competing claims
of the antagonists. Paradoxically, this desire to maintain
a morally neutral stance between them was to create a
big problem for Anouilh in 1944. That he should have
been surprised by it in the context of the German
Occupation points to a degree of innocence in him
worthy of his heroine.

The play opened on 4 February 1944 at the Théâtre
de l'Atelier on the Right Bank in Paris. André Barsacq
directed; Anouilh's wife Monelle Valentin played
Antigone, Jean Davy Créon, and Auguste Bovério the
Prologue-Chorus. This was at a time when the tide was
beginning to turn against the Germans militarily on
many fronts. But although life was still harsh and
perilous in Nazi-occupied France, theatre performances
and cultural activity generally had been encouraged
throughout the war, no doubt for propaganda reasons,
by the Germans and the collaborators. Despite
transport problems, curfews and lack of heating, the
theatre was well supported by audiences, although
performances often took place in less than ideal
circumstances, due to power cuts and air-raid warnings,
etc. Production budgets were minimal, and materials
for sets and costumes were in short supply. The
consequence of this was far from a disaster: *Antigone*
was not the only play at this time for which a simple,
neutral set and austere, uncomplicated costumes were
prescribed. Nothing got in the way of dramatic
essentials, and this could be an artistic virtue.

Just like Sartre's *The Flies* a year earlier, *Antigone* was
seen as a Greek play with a thinly disguised message
for the French. At first, certain of Anouilh's
compatriots hostile to collaboration with the Germans
interpreted *Antigone* as a play with a meaning for a
country suffering under alien rule: like Orestes in *The
Flies*, was not Antigone an incarnation of the spirit of
resistance to tyranny, if not a coded encouragement to

the French Resistance? This was a plausible
interpretation of Antigone's stubborn defiance and self-
sacrifice. It might seem a matter for congratulation then
that Anouilh, like Sartre before him, had appeared to
pull the wool over the eyes of the German censor.

However, the anti-collaborationist meaning was not
the only one to be decoded from *Antigone* in the
context of the Occupation. The play had been
authorised for performance without difficulty shortly
after its completion in 1942, and the German bureau of
censorship had no second thoughts during the play's
long run of some five hundred performances. The
reason is not difficult to find: the Germans and their
eager French collaborators also had ways of interpreting
Antigone's defiance, and they were actually quite
pleased with the play. Alain Laubreaux, a leading
theatre reviewer in *Je suis partout* and a notorious
collaborator who met a grim fate at the Liberation,
spoke for many when he admired Antigone's thirst for
a world of purity but denounced her way of trying to
achieve it. It could lead only to 'chaos, disorder and
suicide'. His colleague Charles Méré in *Aujourd'hui*
could find nothing to admire in her, and denounced
her in stronger language still: Antigone was a
'degenerate, unintelligent madwoman whose revolt
produces only anarchy, disaster and death'.

In fact the Germans and the collaborators had an
even better reason for being pleased to see *Antigone* run
and run: Creon is portrayed very favourably by
Anouilh. Méré put it in a nutshell: 'The real hero is
Creon, the just ruler, a slave to his duty who sacrifices
everything that is dear to him for the sake of his
country.' This was exactly the kind of case that
collaborators had put for Marshal Pétain since 1940.
Just as Anouilh's Creon had not wanted to become
king of Thebes and would have preferred to be left in
peace with his books, Pétain, it was argued, had come
out of a well-earned retirement to save France from

chaos; collaboration was just a sad necessity, a way of sparing France from a worse fate if the Germans were provoked. At the same time, another side to Anouilh's Creon, his wheeling-dealing, cynical, political pragmatism, reminded many of Pierre Laval, a fervent pro-Nazi who had been Pétain's Prime Minister during much of the Occupation. Anouilh's Creon was soon interpreted as an amalgam of these two figures in the clandestine press in the spring of 1944, before being denounced in Gaullist as well as communist publications once France was liberated. When a fresh production of *Antigone* was mounted in September 1944, much hostility was directed towards Anouilh and André Barsacq, because the play was considered to be an apologia for the Collaboration. It obviously did not help matters that the play had been so well reviewed by the collaborationist press.

In the years immediately following the Liberation Anouilh had to endure further criticism. As recounted in the Chronology to this edition, he threw fuel on the flames by involving himself in a futile campaign for clemency for Robert Brasillach, a convicted collaborator who was sentenced to death and shot in 1945. Yet the controversy over *Antigone* never caused him to be cited for investigation during the '*épuration*' (purges of collaborators). It was not easy to pin much on him. *Antigone* is a thoroughly ambiguous play after all. Anouilh's portrayal of Creon as an emergency leader driven to ruthless methods in a crisis is admittedly indulgent, but can that crisis as painted by the author be said to provoke those who had resisted the Collaboration? Creon is given no Laval-type diatribes about Jews, intellectuals, Anglo-American capitalists, trade union leaders, international Marxist conspiracies, the Popular Front of 1936, etc. And he is clearly shown to have some unsavoury henchmen under him. The uncouth guards in their black gear are as near as Anouilh could have gone in 1944 to paint an oblique

picture of the sinister Vichyite militia, and he puts no
moral or political case for them whatsoever. So no
official sanction came Anouilh's way. He was left in
peace, to be permanently detested by the French left,
and increasingly at home with the bourgeoisie. The
latter became his faithful public and in great numbers
supported play after play after the war, sometimes with
three running at the same time, when the new
productions of *Antigone* are included, which took place
in 1947, 1949, 1950 and 1953.

Antigone's first translation to the English-speaking
world was in February 1946 at the Cort Theatre, New
York. *Thieves' Carnival* had been performed successfully
in New York as early as 1938 (and was frequently
revived). Although not very well known in the United
States, by 1946 Anouilh was beginning to be thought of
as the author of bitter-sweet (black/pink) comedies,
with an audience preference for the pink end of the
spectrum. So anyone looking to *Antigone* for the
quintessence of French frothiness, boulevard chic, could
only be disappointed. The play did not go down well,
and closed after only forty-four performances. Lewis
Falb (*Jean Anouilh*) considers that, despite the big
name of Cedric Hardwicke in the role of Creon, the
failure might in part have been due to the perverse
casting of a fifty-year-old actress, Katharine Cornell, in
the role of Antigone. Corsets and makeup can achieve
only so much. But there is more than just that. Critics
complained of the 'wordiness' and abstraction of the
play, and the existential theme appears to have left
them indifferent; the German Occupation of France
must have seemed a long way away. Also the self-
conscious Pirandellian framing by the Prologue-Chorus
was alien to the naturalist structures in which American
audiences at that time expected heavyweight moral
dramas to be set – Arthur Miller was waiting in the
wings: *Death of a Salesman* was always going to be at
the very least a more substantial evening's theatre than

Death of a Greek (or French?) Adolescent.

By the middle nineteen-sixties American expectations of what Anouilh had to offer were transformed for the better, as a result of the Broadway successes of *The Lark* in 1955 and *Becket* in 1960, the latter starring Laurence Olivier and Anthony Quinn. Even then, at the American Shakespeare Festival Theater at Stratford, Connecticut, *Antigone* fared no better: 'The play failed once again to find critical approval. Francis Herridge's comments in the *Post* were typical: she called *Antigone* an unsatisfying, even exasperating theater work' (Falb, p.69).

Antigone had to wait three years longer to make its debut in London, and it had a better fate. In 1949 Anouilh had the good fortune to have his play performed by London's most prestigious company for new theatre work, the Old Vic, led by Sir Laurence Olivier and his wife Vivien Leigh, probably by then the most famous couple in the English-speaking theatre world. The play, in Lewis Galantière's translation, opened on 10 February at the Old Vic's home, the New Theatre. It was part of a double-bill. Chekhov's *The Proposal* was the curtain-raiser, a farce played at breakneck speed that got the evening off to a racing, if somewhat inappropriate, start. Reviews of *Antigone* were unfailingly good. They ranged from the ecstatic to the grudgingly complimentary – not everyone in those austere years in Britain was enchanted by the living legend of 'the Oliviers' (but one person who had no doubts was Queen Mary, whose visit to the Old Vic was the third of the week: things were different then).

Olivier directed and took what for any other actor of that time would have been the lesser role of the Chorus. He relished every demonstrative second of it, darting about the stage like an enthusiastic lecturer; his famed diction was as impeccable as his white shirt and tails. The popular actor George Relph in the role of Creon gave 'the performance of his career' (*Yorkshire*

Post). The reviewers' main focus was naturally
Antigone, played by Vivien Leigh, 'superb',
'magnificent', 'like a woman set apart', etc. She was
described as intense and deeply moving throughout,
although a few reviewers thought she just lacked fire
and a variation in vocal range at the moment of angry
rebellion. Finally, Richard Findlater in his review for
Theatre found it exasperating that 'the most beautiful
woman on the English stage should have to doggedly
assert her ugliness'.

Vivien Leigh's costume was dark green, so a cue was
not taken here from Barsacq's Paris production, in
which costume design was themed in black and white
to good effect. In other ways as well, Olivier's
production regarded itself as not bound to follow the
French design precedent or indeed Anouilh's
description of the set as 'neutral' (not translated by
Galantière). A classical portico is prominent, the guards
wear vaguely ancient helmets. Perhaps predictably, and
much applauded, the guard Jonas (Thomas Heathcote)
had a cockney accent – or what passed for such on the
London stage in 1949. A curiosity of all these reviews is
that the minuscule role of the messenger (Terence
Morgan) is singled out for praise often, Ismene (Meg
Maxwell) and Haemon (Dan Cunningham) virtually
never.

One review (*Sunday Times*, 13 February) is
significant for situating the play in its contemporary
dramatic context, with Anouilh being associated with
Albert Camus and Jean-Paul Sartre in writing
challenging 'existential' plays about the necessity of
choice. The reviewer was Harold Hobson, soon to be
the author of a study that was useful in its time, *The
French Theatre of Today*, (1953). As for the other
reviews, despite reservations about the anachronisms –
those clever French at it again – it was a common
theme of them that no sense of incongruity (the usual
word) persisted long. The political context of the

Occupation was perceived, and the parallels accepted without much comment. The sniffiness of the *Daily Mail* reviewer ('this play so essentially gallic in its cynicism') was the exception rather than the rule. On the whole *Antigone* received a sympathetic welcome in 1949 from London reviewers and theatre-goers. They were close enough to the French to be nostalgic about the Resistance ethos (and receptive to its continued propagation), not so close as to be divided and enraged by Anouilh's gloss on it.

In the course of time, in France as well as elsewhere, the context of the German Occupation receded into the past, and productions of *Antigone* since then have tended towards a more generalised climate of youthful idealism on the one hand and the political opportunism and cynicism of the adult world on the other. The play lends itself *approximately* to particular contexts, if relocated in a country badly affected by civil war or some similar type of polarising conflict. Thus it was performed in 1959 at the Festival of Mers-el-Kebir in an Algeria that was in the process of being torn apart by a savage war for independence. As is clear from a very evocative photograph in the Monférier edition of the play (Bordas, 1968, p.32), that production was very much a part of the doomed culture of the European community making up only ten per cent of the country's population. What little division there was in that *pied noir* minority about the wisdom or otherwise of trying to hang on to Algeria polarised on old-fashioned left–right ideological lines (with the left far outnumbered). If any Europeans had their conscience disturbed in some way by the play – and 1959 was the year when the French army was acknowledged to be using systematic torture to counter the Algerian insurgents' (FLN) terrorism – there is no evidence that they were of Antigone's generation. The young are not invariably on the side of the angels.

Antigone as a dramatic text for both study and

performance is one of the few survivors of the great age
of French theatre that extended from 1930 to 1960. It
is still being performed somewhere in the world long
after the names of Pétain and Laval have been
forgotten. With the bitter evidence that confronts them
at the beginning of the third millennium, a new
generation of performers, students as well as
professionals, would not be human if they did not yield
to the temptation to re-contextualise the play. Enough
devastated cities and provinces are proof of the folly of
unchecked political power. But in the end no
production can get round the fact that a close reading
of *Antigone* will always reveal the importance of the
theme of childhood. The heroine is the victim of a
personal trauma – not shared by any others of her
generation in the play – about leaving behind that state
of innocence and security. Antigone's *solipsistic* vision,
her fundamentally Romantic individualism that prevents
her from compromising with the looming demands of
the adult world, has to be reconciled with, but not
subordinated to, a commitment to an act of defiance
incurring the direst penalty. This may be 'only an
excuse' – we must always entertain the suspicion that
Anouilh, unlike Sophocles, means us to feel Creon is
right. It does not prevent us from regarding Antigone
as a deeply moving heroine. Giving full artistic
expression to the ambiguity of Antigone's motivation is
the challenge that confronted Anouilh's eminent
director André Barsacq in 1944; this challenge will not
go away.

Further Reading

Sophocles, *Antigone*, trs. Don Taylor, in *Sophocles: Plays One* (Methuen, London, 1986)

Editions of *Antigone* in French

Antigone, La Table Ronde, Paris, 1946

Antigone in *Nouvelles Pièces noires*, La Table Ronde, Paris, 1946

Antigone, ed. W.M. Landers, Harrap, London, 1954 (a slightly bowdlerised edition, with introduction and notes in English)

Antigone, ed. R. Laubreaux, Didier, Paris, 1964

Antigone, ed. J. Monférier, Bordas, Paris, 1968 (an abridged edition with excellent commentary and notes in French)

Books and articles on *Antigone*

Etienne Frois, *Antigone: Profil d'une oeuvre*, Hatier, Paris, 1972

William D. Howarth, *Anouilh: Antigone,* Edward Arnold, London, 1983

Walter N. Ince, 'Prologue and Chorus in Anouilh's *Antigone*', *Forum for Modern Language Studies*, IV, 1968, pp. 277–84

Murray Sachs, 'Notes on the Theatricality of Jean Anouilh's *Antigone*', *French Review*, XXXVI, 1962, pp. 3–11

Books and articles on Anouilh

Jean Anouilh, *La Vicomtesse d'Eristal n'a pas reçu son balai mécanique: Souvenirs d'un jeune homme*, La Table Ronde, 1987

Marguerite Archer, *Jean Anouilh*, Columbia University Press, New York, 1971

Bernard Beugnot (ed.), *Les Critiques de notre temps et Anouilh*, Garnier, Paris, 1977

Clément Borgal, *Anouilh: la peine de vivre*, Centurion, Paris, 1966

Lewis W. Falb, *Jean Anouilh*, Frederick Ungar, New York, 1977

Alba Della Fazia, *Jean Anouilh*, Twayne, New York, 1969

Hubert Gignoux, *Jean Anouilh*, Temps Présent, Paris, 1946

Paul Ginestier, *Jean Anouilh*, Seghers, Paris, 1969

Jacques Guicharnaud, 'From Disappointment to Play: Jean Anouilh' in *Modern French Theatre from Giraudoux to Genet*, Yale University Press, New Haven and London, revised edition, 1975

John Harvey, *Anouilh: a Study in Theatrics*, Yale University Press, New Haven, 1964

William D. Howarth, 'Anouilh', *Forces in Modern French Drama*, ed. J. Fletcher, University of London Press, 1972

Kathleen W. Kelly, *Jean Anouilh: an Annotated Bibliography*, Scarecrow Press, New Jersey, 1973

Robert de Luppé, *Jean Anouilh*, Editions Universitaires, Paris, 1959

Thérèse Malachy, *Jean Anouilh: les problèmes de l'existence dans un théâtre de marionnettes*, Nizet, Paris, 1978

H.G. McIntyre, *The Theatre of Jean Anouilh*, Harrap, London, 1981

Leonard C. Pronko, *The World of Jean Anouilh*, California University Press, Berkeley, 1961

André F. Rombout, *La Pureté dans le théâtre de Jean Anouilh: amour et bonheur ou l'anarchisme réactionnaire*, Holland University Press, Amsterdam, 1975

Philip Thody, *Anouilh*, Oliver and Boyd, Edinburgh, 1968

Paul Vandromme, *Jean Anouilh, un auteur et ses personnages*, La Table Ronde, Paris, 1965

General studies

Lionel Abel, *Metatheatre: A New View of Dramatic Form*, Hill and Wang, New York, 1963

René-Marill Albérès, *La Révolte des écrivains d'aujourd'hui*, Corrêa, Paris, 1949

Leo Aylen, *Greek Tragedy and the Modern World*, Methuen, London, 1964

Angela Belli, 'The Use of Mythological Themes and Characters in 20th Century Drama; Four Approaches', PhD, New York University, 1965; *Dissertation Abstracts*, XXVII, Ann Arbor, Michigan, May 1967

Thomas Bishop, *Pirandello and the French Theatre*, Peter Owen, London, 1961

David Bradby, *Modern French Drama 1940–1990*, Cambridge University Press, Cambridge, 1991

Simone Fraisse, *Le Mythe d'Antigone*, Armand Colin, Paris, 1974

David I. Grossvogel, *The Self-Conscious Stage in Modern French Theatre*, Columbia University Press, New York, 1958

Pat G. Hastings, 'Symbolism in the adaptations of Greek myth by modern French dramatists', *Nottingham French Studies*, 2, 1963, pp. 25–34

S.B. John, 'Obsession and Technique in the Plays of Jean Anouilh', *French Studies*, XI, 1957, pp. 97–116

F.L. Lucas, *Tragedy: Serious Drama in Relation to Aristotle's Poetics*, Hogarth Press, London, 1966

M.F. McFeeters, *The Use of Greek Mythology in the French Theatre from 1914 to 1948*, Syracuse University, 1954

Robert Nelson, *Play within a Play*, Yale University Press, New Haven, 1958

George Steiner, *The Death of Tragedy*, Faber & Faber, London, 1961

Raymond Williams, *Modern Tragedy*, Chatto & Windus, London, 1966

Selected English translations of Anouilh's plays

Anouilh Plays: One, introduced by Ned Chaillet (Methuen, 1991), contains:

> *Antigone*, trs. Barbara Bray, 1987
> *Léocadia*, trs. Timberlake Wertenbaker, 1987
> *The Waltz of the Toreadors* (*La Valse des toréadors*), trs. Lucienne Hill, 1953, revised 1987
> *The Lark* (*L'Alouette*), trs. Christopher Fry, 1955
> *Poor Bitos* (*Pauvre Bitos ou le dîner de têtes*), trs. Lucienne Hill, 1964

Anouilh Plays: Two, introduced by Ned Chaillet (Methuen, 1997), contains:

> *The Rehearsal* (*La Répétition*), trs. Jeremy Sams, 1991
> *Becket* (*Becket ou l'honneur de Dieu*), trs. Jeremy Sams, 1997
> *Eurydice*, trs. Peter Meyer, 1997
> *The Orchestra* (*L'Orchestre*), trs. Jeremy Sams, 1997

Traveller without Luggage (*Le Voyageur sans bagage*), trs. John Whiting (Samuel French, 1959)

Restless Heart (*La Sauvage*), trs. Lucienne Hill (Methuen, 1957)

Thieves' Carnival (*Le Bal des voleurs*), trs. Lucienne Hill (Methuen, 1952)

Dinner with the Family (*Le Rendez-vous de Senlis*), trs. Edward Owen Marsh (Samuel French, 1958; Methuen, 1958)

Ring Round the Moon (*L'Invitation au château*), trs. Christopher Fry (Methuen, 1950; Samuel French, 1976)

Ardèle (*Ardèle ou la marguerite*), trs. Lucienne Hill, published with *Colombe* (Methuen, 1959)

The Cavern (*La Grotte*), trs. Lucienne Hill (Hill and Wang, New York, 1966)

The Fighting Cock (*L'Hurluberlu, ou Le Réactionnaire amoureux*), trs. Lucienne Hill (Methuen, 1967)

Dear Antoine (*Cher Antoine*), trs. Lucienne Hill (Hill and Wang, New York, 1971)

The Director of the Opera (*Le Directeur de l'Opéra*), trs. Lucienne Hill (Methuen, 1973)

Number One (*Le Nombril*), trs. Michael Frayn (Samuel French, 1986)

Antigone

translated by
Barbara Bray

Characters

PROLOGUE-CHORUS
CREON, *King of Thebes*
ANTIGONE, *his niece*
ISMENE, *sister of Antigone*
HAEMON, *son of Creon*
NURSE
MESSENGER
JONAS, *first guard*
BINNS, *second guard*
SNOUT, *third guard*
EURYDICE, *Queen of Thebes*
PAGE

Set without historical or geographical implications. Three identical doors. At curtain rise all the characters are onstage, chatting, knitting, playing cards, and so on. The PROLOGUE *emerges from the rest and comes forward to* speak.

PROLOGUE. The people gathered here are about to act the story of Antigone. The one who's going to play the lead is the thin girl sitting there silent. Staring in front of her. Thinking. She's thinking that soon she's going to be Antigone. That she'll suddenly stop being the thin dark girl whose family didn't take her seriously, and rise up alone against everyone. Against Creon, her uncle . . . the king. She's thinking she's going to die . . . though she's still young, and like everyone else would have preferred to live.

But there's nothing to be done. Her name is Antigone, and she's going to have to play her part right through to the end.

Ever since the play started she has felt herself hurtling further and further away from her sister Ismene. (That's her, chatting and laughing with a young man over there.) Further and further away from all the rest of us, who are just here to watch, and haven't got to die in a few hours' time.

The young man talking to Ismene – fair-haired, beautiful, happy Ismene – is Haemon, son of Creon. He is Antigone's fiancé. Everything combined to attract him to Ismene – his love of dancing and sport, of happiness and success. His senses too, for Ismene is

much prettier than Antigone. And then one evening,
when there was a ball and he'd been dancing every
dance with Ismene, dazzling in a new gown, he went
and sought out Antigone where she sat dreaming in a
corner, as she is now, with her arms clasped round her
knees. And he asked her to be his wife. She looked up
at him with those sober eyes of hers, unsurprised,
smiled a sad little smile . . . and said 'yes'. The
orchestra struck up again, Ismene was there across the
room, in peals of laughter among the young men . . .
and now he, Haemon, was going to be Antigone's
husband. He didn't know that never in this world would
there be such a person as Antigone's husband. That all
this princely title conferred on him was the right to die.

The vigorous grey-haired man deep in thought, his
young page beside him, is Creon, the king. He is
wrinkled, tired. He is playing a difficult game: he has
become a leader of men. Before, in the reign of
Oedipus, when Creon was only the most influential man
at court, he loved music and fine bindings, would spend
hours prowling round Thebes's little antique shops. But
Oedipus and his sons are dead. And Creon, forsaking
his books and his collector's pieces, has rolled up his
sleeves and taken their place. Sometimes, in the
evening, when he's worn out, he wonders whether it's
not pointless, being a leader of men. Whether it's not a
sordid business that ought to be left to others less . . ·
sensitive than himself. Then, next morning, he's faced
with particular problems to be solved, and he just gets
up without more ado, like a labourer starting a day's
work.

The old woman winding wool by the fireplace is the
Nurse who brought up the two girls, and the elderly
lady beside her, busy with her knitting, is Eurydice,
Creon's wife. She'll go on knitting right through the

tragedy, until it's her turn to stand up and die. She is kind, dignified, loving. She is of no help to Creon. He is alone. Alone with his little page who is too small and can't be of any help to him either.

The pale youth alone on the other side of the room, leaning pensively against the wall, is the Messenger. He's the one who will in due course come and tell of Haemon's death. That's why he doesn't feel like talking and laughing with the others. He knows . . .

Lastly, those three red-faced fellows playing cards, with their caps pushed back on their heads – they're the guards. Not bad chaps. They've got wives . . . children . . . little worries the same as everyone else. But before long they'll be collaring the accused without turning a hair. They smell of garlic and leather and red wine, and are completely devoid of imagination. They are the agents – eternally innocent, eternally complacent – of justice. For the time being the justice they serve is the justice of Creon . . . until the day comes when Thebes designates Creon's successor, and they are ordered to arrest Creon himself.

And now that you know them all they can act out their story. It begins when Oedipus's two sons, who were supposed to rule Thebes alternately, each for one year turn and turn about, fought and slew each other outside the city walls because Eteocles, the elder, refused to give way to his brother Polynices after his first year in power. Seven great foreign princes whom Polynices had won over to his case were defeated also at the city's seven gates. Now Thebes is safe, the two rival brothers are dead, and Creon the king has decreed that Eteocles, the virtuous brother, will be given an elaborate funeral, while Polynices, the good-for-nothing, the rebel, will be left unburied and unwept, a prey to ravens and jackals. Anyone affording him proper burial rites will be mercilessly punished, with death.

While the PROLOGUE *was speaking the other characters
have left the stage one by one. Then the* PROLOGUE
*too disappears. The light, meanwhile, has turned to
that of a grey dawn in a sleeping house.* ANTIGONE
*quietly opens the door and tiptoes in from outside,
carrying her shoes in her hand. She stands still and
listens. The* NURSE *appears.*

NURSE. Where have you been?

ANTIGONE. Just out for a walk. It was all grey. Beautiful.
But now everything's turned pink and yellow and green.
Like a postcard. You'll have to get up earlier, Nan, if
you want to see a world without colours.

She makes as if to go.

NURSE. Not so fast! I was up while it was still pitch dark! I
went to your room to make sure you hadn't thrown the
blankets off in your sleep . . . and the bed was empty!

ANTIGONE. The garden was still asleep. I caught it
unawares. A garden that hasn't yet begun to think
about people. Beautiful.

NURSE. I soon saw you'd gone out – you'd left the back
door open.

ANTIGONE. The fields were all wet. Waiting. Everything
was waiting. I made a terrific noise all by myself on the
road, and I felt awkward because I knew the waiting
wasn't for me. So I took my sandals off and melted into
the landscape . . .

NURSE. You're going to have to wash those feet before
you get back into bed.

ANTIGONE. I'm not going back to bed.

NURSE. Four o'clock. It wasn't even four o'clock yet! I get

up to make sure she's still properly covered up, and there's her bed cold, and nobody in it!

ANTIGONE. Do you think it would be like that every morning, being the first girl out?

NURSE. Morning! Middle of the night, you mean! And are you trying to tell me you were only out for a walk? Story-teller! Where've you been?

ANTIGONE (*with a strange smile*). You're right. It was still night. I was the only one out there who thought it was morning. The first person today to believe in the light.

NURSE. Go on then – play the fool. I'm up to all your tricks – I was young once myself, and I was a handful too. Now tell me where you've been, you naughty girl!

ANTIGONE (*suddenly serious*). I wasn't doing anything wrong.

NURSE. You had a rendezvous, I suppose – don't tell me you hadn't!

ANTIGONE (*quietly*). Yes, I had a rendezvous.

NURSE. You mean you've got a sweetheart?

Pause.

ANTIGONE (*strangely*). Yes . . . Poor thing.

NURSE (*angry*). A nice thing for a king's daughter, I must say! You half kill yourself to bring them up, but they're all the same . . . And yet you used not to be like the others, preening in front of the glass and putting rouge on their lips and trying to attract attention. The times I've said to myself, 'My goodness, this child isn't vain enough! For ever in the same dress, with her hair all over the place – the lads'll all be after Ismene with her curls and her ribbons, and this one'll be left on my hands!' And all the time you were just like your sister –

worse, you little hypocrite! . . . Who is it? Some young layabout, I suppose? A boy you can't even introduce to your family as the one you love and want to marry? That's it, isn't it? . . . Isn't it? Answer me, you brazen hussy!

   Pause.

ANTIGONE (*with a faint smile again*). Yes, Nurse. That's it.

NURSE. 'Yes', she says! Heaven help us! I've had her since she was a tiny tot, I promised her mother I'd make a respectable young woman of her – and now look! But you haven't heard the last of this, my girl! I may only be your nurse, and you may treat me like an old fool, but your uncle Creon's going to find out about this I can tell you!

ANTIGONE (*suddenly weary*). Yes, Nan. I know. Leave me alone now.

NURSE. And do you know what he's going to say when he hears about you getting up in the middle of the night? And what about Haemon, your fiancé? She's engaged, and she gets up at four in the morning to gad about with someone else! And then she wants to be left alone – her highness doesn't want anyone to say anything about it! Do you know what I ought to do? I ought to give you a good spanking, like when you were a little girl.

ANTIGONE. Don't make a fuss, Nan. You oughtn't to be too cross this morning.

NURSE. Not make a fuss! When I think how I promised her mother . . .! What would she say if she were here? 'You silly old fool,' she'd say – 'so you couldn't keep my little girl virtuous for me! For ever fussing over them with cardigans so they shan't catch cold and egg custards to build up their strength. But at four in the morning, when you're really needed, you're sleeping like a log, you who claim you never get a wink all night, so you let them slip out of the house as easy as pie, and when you get there the bed's stone cold!' That's what your mother'll say to me up there, when I go. And I'll be so ashamed I could die, if I wasn't dead already, and all I'll be able to do is hang my head and say, 'Yes, Lady Jocasta – you're absolutely right.'

ANTIGONE. Stop crying, Nan. You'll be able to look her straight in the eye, and she'll thank you for taking such good care of me. She knows why I went out this morning.

NURSE. You haven't got a sweetheart?

ANTIGONE. No.

NURSE. So you've been making fun of me? I suppose it's because I'm old. You were always my favourite. And though your sister was easier to manage, I thought it was you who loved me best, too. But if you did love me you'd have told me the truth. Why was the bed empty when I came to tuck you in?

ANTIGONE. Please don't cry. (*She kisses her.*) Come along, my little old red apple. Do you remember when I used to rub your cheeks till they shone? Don't fill all these little furrows with tears for nothing. I am virtuous, I swear I have no other sweetheart than Haemon. If you like, I'll swear I never shall. Save your tears – you may have need of them. When you cry I feel like a little girl again. And I mustn't be little today.

Enter ISMENE.

ISMENE. Up already, Antigone? I went to your room and –

ANTIGONE. Yes. I'm up already.

NURSE. So do the pair of you mean to start getting up in

the morning before the servants? What sort of behaviour is that for princesses? Strolling about before breakfast . . . not even properly dressed. You'll both be catching colds on me again before –

ANTIGONE. It's summer now, Nan – we shall be all right. Go and make us some coffee, won't you? (*She sits down, tired suddenly.*) I could do with a cup.

NURSE. My dove! There she is, light-headed for want of something to eat, and I stand here like a fool . . .

She hurries off.

ISMENE. Don't you feel well?

ANTIGONE. It's nothing. Just a bit tired. (*Smiling.*) That comes of getting up so early.

ISMENE. I couldn't sleep either.

ANTIGONE (*smiling*). But you must, or you won't be so pretty in the morning.

ISMENE. Don't make fun.

ANTIGONE. I'm not. It's a comfort to me this morning, your being pretty. Do you remember how miserable it used to make me when I was little? How I used to daub you with mud and put worms down your neck? And once I tied you to a tree and cut off your hair! (*Stroking* ISMENE's *hair.*) Such beautiful hair . . . How easy it must be not to have foolish thoughts, with all these lovely sleek locks hanging round your head!

ISMENE (*abruptly*). Why have you changed the subject?

ANTIGONE (*gently, still stroking* ISMENE's *hair*). I haven't . . .

ISMENE. Listen, Antigone. I've been thinking . . .

ANTIGONE. Yes . . . ?

ISMENE. Turning it over in my mind all night . . . You're mad.

ANTIGONE. That's right.

ISMENE. We can't do it!

Pause.

ANTIGONE (*in her usual quiet voice*). Why not?

ISMENE. They'll kill us!

ANTIGONE. Of course they will. Everyone has his part to play. Creon has to have us put to death, and we have to go and bury our brother. That's how the cast-list was drawn up. What can we do about it?

ISMENE. I don't want to die!

ANTIGONE (*quietly*). I'd have preferred not to.

ISMENE. Listen. I'm older than you, and not so impulsive. You do the first thing that comes into your head, never mind whether it's sensible or stupid. But I'm more level-headed. I think.

ANTIGONE. Sometimes it's best not to think too much.

ISMENE. I disagree. It's a horrible business, of course, and I feel sorry for Polynices too. But I do see Creon's point of view.

ANTIGONE. I don't want to see it.

ISMENE. He's the king. He has to set an example.

ANTIGONE. But I'm not the king, and I don't! Antigone, self-willed little beast, does the first thing that comes into her head! So then she's stood in the corner or locked up in the dark. And serve her right! She should do as she's told!

ISMENE. That's right! Scowl! Glare! Hold forth without letting anyone else get a word in edgeways! But listen to what I say. I'm right more often than you are.

ANTIGONE. I don't want to be right!

ISMENE . At least try to understand!

ANTIGONE. Understand! You've always been on at me about that, all of you, ever since I was little. I was supposed to understand I mustn't play with water – beautiful, cool, elusive water – because it made the floor wet. Or with earth, because it dirtied my clothes. I was supposed to understand you mustn't eat your cake before you've finished your bread and butter, or give all your pocket-money away to a beggar, or run in the wind till you drop, or drink when you're hot, or go swimming just when you feel like it. Understand, understand, always understand! I don't want to understand! I can do that when I'm old. (*Softly*.) If I ever am.

ISMENE . He's the king, Antigone. He's stronger than we are. And everyone agrees with him. The streets of Thebes are full of them.

ANTIGONE. I'm not listening.

ISMENE . They'll hiss and boo. They'll seize us in their thousand arms, surround us with their thousand faces and their one expression, spit at us. And we'll have to ride in the tumbril through their hatred, through their smell and their laughter to our execution. The guards will be waiting there, with their stupid faces all red from their stiff collars, their great clean hypocrites' hands, their loutish stare. You can shout till you're hoarse, trying to explain – they'll do exactly as they're told, slavishly, without knowing or caring whether it's right or wrong. And the suffering, have you thought of that? We'll have to suffer, feel the pain increasing, mounting up till it's no longer bearable. It has to stop, but it goes on, climbing higher and higher like an ear-splitting shriek . . . I can't! I can't!

ANTIGONE. That's what thinking does for you!

ISMENE . Haven't you thought about it?

ANTIGONE. Yes, of course.

ISMENE . But I'm not brave.

ANTIGONE (*quietly*). Neither am I. What's that got to do with it?

Pause.

ISMENE . Don't you want to live then?

ANTIGONE (*low*). Not want to live . . . (*Lower still if that's possible.*) Who used to be up first in the morning just to feel the chill air on her bare skin? Who used to go to bed last, and then only when she was ready to drop, just so as to live a little bit more of the night? Who used to cry, as a child, because there were so many insects and plants in the fields that it was impossible to collect them all?

ISMENE (*suddenly drawn to her*). Antigone . . . my pet . . .

ANTIGONE (*pulling herself together, crying out*). No! Leave me alone! Now's not the time to be whimpering and putting our arms round one another! You say you've thought things over? And you've come to the conclusion that it's too much – to have the whole city howling for your blood, the pain, the fear of dying?

ISMENE (*hanging her head low*). Yes.

ANTIGONE. Excuses! You can make use of them if you like.

ISMENE (*throwing herself at* ANTIGONE). Antigone! Please! It's all right for men to die for their ideas. But you're a girl.

ANTIGONE (*through clenched teeth*). Only a girl! The tears

I've shed because of it!

ISMENE . Your happiness is within your grasp – you've only to stretch out your hand and take it . . . You're engaged, you're young, you're beautiful . . .

ANTIGONE (*dully*). No – not beautiful.

ISMENE . Yes, in your own way! You know very well it's you the boys turn to look at in the street, you the little girls stare at speechless till you disappear round the corner . . .

ANTIGONE (*faint smile*). Boys in the street . . . Little girls . . .

Pause.

ISMENE . And Haemon? What about Haemon, Antigone?

ANTIGONE (*expressionless*). I'll be talking to him. I'll soon settle him.

ISMENE . You're out of your mind.

ANTIGONE (*smiling*). You've always said that about everything I've ever done . . . Go back to bed, Ismene. It's getting light – look! – and there's nothing I can do. My dead brother's surrounded by guards now, just as if he'd managed to make himself king. Go back to bed. You're pale from lack of sleep.

ISMENE . Aren't you coming?

ANTIGONE . I don't feel like sleeping. But I promise I'll stay here until you wake up. Nurse will bring me something to eat. You go now – you can hardly keep your eyes open.

ISMENE . You will let me talk to you again? Try to make you see . . . ?

ANTIGONE (*with a tinge of weariness*). Yes, yes . . . I'll let you talk to me. I'll let you all talk to me. Go to bed now, please, or you won't be so pretty tomorrow.

She smiles sadly as she watches ISMENE *go, then, suddenly weary, collapses on a chair. Pause.*

Poor Ismene!

Enter NURSE.

NURSE. Here's a nice cup of coffee and some toast, my pigeon. Eat it all up now.

ANTIGONE. I'm not very hungry.

NURSE. I buttered the toast with my own hands, just the way you like it!

ANTIGONE. Thank you, Nan ... I'll just sip some coffee ...

Pause.

NURSE. You're not well, my love. Where does it hurt?

ANTIGONE. Nowhere, Nan. But cuddle me and keep me warm just the same, like you used to when I was ill ... Dear old Nan – stronger than fever or nightmares, stronger than the shadow of the wardrobe, grinning and changing shape on the wall. Stronger than all the insects gnawing away at something in the dark. Stronger than the dark itself, full of crazy shrieks that no one listens to. Stronger than death. Hold my hand, like when you used to come and sit by my bed.

NURSE. What's the matter, my little dove?

ANTIGONE. Nothing, Nan. Just that I'm still a bit small for it all.

NURSE. A bit small for what, my sparrow?

ANTIGONE. Nothing. Anyway, you're here, I'm holding the rough hand that's always kept me safe from everything. Perhaps it will keep me safe still.

NURSE. What can I do for you, my turtle dove?

ANTIGONE. Just rest your hand on my cheek – like this. (*She keeps her eyes closed for a moment.*) There, I'm not afraid any more. Not of the wicked ogre, nor of the bogey man, nor of the Pied Piper. (*Pause. Change of tone.*) Nurse, you know Floss . . . ?

NURSE. Don't talk to me about that blessed dog. Pawmarks over everything. Oughtn't to be allowed in the house.

ANTIGONE. Promise you won't grumble at her any more. Even if she leaves pawmarks everywhere.

NURSE. You mean I'm to let her ruin everything and not say a word?

ANTIGONE. Yes.

NURSE. No, that's too much – !

ANTIGONE. You're quite fond of her really. And you enjoy polishing and scrubbing – you wouldn't like it if everything was always spick and span . . .

NURSE. What if she wets my carpets?

ANTIGONE. Promise not to scold her even then. Please, Nan.

NURSE. You know how to get round people, don't you?

ANTIGONE. And I want you to talk to her too.

NURSE (*shrugging*). Talk to brute beasts!

ANTIGONE. Not as if she's a brute beast! As I do . . . As if she were a real person.

NURSE. Play the fool like that at my age? But why?

ANTIGONE (*gently*). Well, if for some reason or other I couldn't talk to her myself any more.

NURSE (*not understanding*). What do you mean? Why not?

ANTIGONE (*first looking away, then in a harsher voice*). But if she's too miserable . . . if she keeps waiting with her nose glued to the door like when I go out without her – then perhaps it would be best to have her put to sleep.

NURSE. Have Floss put to sleep? Whatever's the matter with you this morning?

Enter HAEMON.

ANTIGONE. Here's Haemon. Leave us, Nan. And don't forget what you promised.

Exit NURSE.

ANTIGONE (*running over to* HAEMON). Forgive me for quarrelling yesterday evening, Haemon. And for everything. It was my fault. Please forgive me.

HAEMON. You know I'd forgiven you as soon as you'd gone out and slammed the door! The perfume you were wearing was still in the air, and I'd forgiven you already. (*He takes her in his arms, smiles, looks at her.*) Who did you steal it from, that scent?

ANTIGONE. Ismene.

HAEMON. And the lipstick, the powder, the pretty dress?

ANTIGONE. Ismene.

HAEMON. And what was it all in aid of?

ANTIGONE. I'll tell you presently. (*She nestles closer to him*). Oh, my darling, how stupid I've been! A whole beautiful evening wasted.

HAEMON. There'll be others.

ANTIGONE. Will there?

HAEMON. Other quarrels too. Happiness is full of them.

ANTIGONE. Happiness . . . Listen, Haemon.

HAEMON. Yes, Antigone.

ANTIGONE. Don't laugh this morning. Be serious.

HAEMON. I am serious.

ANTIGONE. And hold me tight. Tighter than ever before. Give me all your strength.

HAEMON. There . . . All my strength . . .

ANTIGONE. Ah . . . (*They remain silent for a moment.*) Haemon, you know the little boy we would have had . . . ?

HAEMON. Yes.

ANTIGONE. You know I'd have shielded him against everything?

HAEMON. Yes.

ANTIGONE. I'd have held him so tight he'd never have been afraid – not of the creeping dark, nor of the unmoving sun, nor of the shadows. He'd have had an unkempt, skinny little mother, but one who was safer than all the real mothers put together, with their real bosoms and their nice big aprons! You believe me, don't you?

HAEMON. Yes, my love.

ANTIGONE. And you do believe you'd have had a real wife?

HAEMON (*holding her*). I've got one already.

ANTIGONE. Oh Haemon, you did love me that evening, didn't you?

HAEMON (*gently*). Which evening?

ANTIGONE. You are sure, aren't you, that when you came and found me at the dance, you didn't pick the wrong girl? You're sure you've never regretted it, never

thought – even deep down, even once – that you ought
really to have asked Ismene?

HAEMON. Don't be silly!

ANTIGONE. You do love me, don't you? Your arms don't
lie, nor the smell of you, nor this heavenly warmth, nor
the confidence that fills me when I lean my head on
your shoulder?

HAEMON. Yes, Antigone. I love you.

ANTIGONE I'm so dark and thin. Ismene's pink and gold
like an apricot.

HAEMON (*low*). Antigone . . .

ANTIGONE. Oh, I'm making myself blush. But this
morning I must know. When you think how I'm going
to be yours, do you feel a great void growing inside you,
as if something were dying?

HAEMON. Yes.

ANTIGONE. So do I. And I want you to know I'd have been
proud to be your wife, the one whose shoulder you'd
have patted absent-mindedly as you sat down in the
evening, as if you were patting something that was truly
yours. (*She moves away from him and speaks in a
different tone of voice.*) So. Now two things. And when
you've heard them you must go away without asking
any questions. Even if they seem strange. Even if they
give you pain.

HAEMON. But what can they be?

ANTIGONE. Promise you'll go without even a backward
glance. If you love me, promise. (*She looks at his
shocked, pitiful expression.*) It's the last foolishness
you'll have to forgive me.

   Pause.

HAEMON. I promise.

ANTIGONE. Thank you. Well, to go back to yesterday first.
You asked me just now why I was wearing Ismene's
dress, her perfume and make-up. Well, I was a fool – I
wasn't sure it was me you really wanted, and I was
trying to make you want me by being more like the
other girls.

HAEMON. So that was it!

ANTIGONE. Yes. And you laughed, and we quarrelled. My
bad temper got the better of me and I flounced off.
(*Pause. Lower.*) But I really came to see you yesterday
evening so that you might make love to me – so that I
might be your wife already. Before . . . (*He draws back
and is about to speak, but she cries out.*) You promised
not to ask! (*Humbly.*) Please . . . (*Turning away;
harshly.*) Anyway, let me explain. I wanted to become
your wife because that's how I love you . . . And
because – forgive me for hurting you, my darling –
because I can never marry you.

   *He is dumbfounded. She runs over to the window and
   cries out.*

Haemon, you promised! Go now. If you speak, or take
one step towards me I'll jump out of this window. I
swear it on the head of the son we had in our dreams.
The only son I'll ever have. Go now, quickly. You'll
understand tomorrow. Soon. (*She sounds so despairing
that* HAEMON *does as she says.*) That's right, Haemon,
leave me. It's the only thing you can do now to show
that you love me.

   HAEMON *has gone.* ANTIGONE *stands still, with her back
   to the audience, then shuts the window and goes and*

sits on a little chair in the middle of the stage. When she speaks she sounds strangely at peace.

There, Antigone. Now Haemon's over and done with.

Enter ISMENE.

ISMENE (*calling*). Oh, you're still here!

ANTIGONE (*not moving*). Why aren't you asleep?

ISMENE. I couldn't sleep. I was so afraid you might go and bury him, even in the light. (*Close.*) Antigone . . . little sister . . . here we all are – Haemon, Nurse, me . . . Floss . . . We love you, we're alive, and we need you! Polynices is dead, and he didn't love you. He was always more a stranger to us than a brother. Forget him, Antigone, as he forgot us! Let Polynices' harsh ghost wander for ever unburied, since that's what Creon decrees. Don't attempt what's beyond your strength. You like to hurl defiance at the whole world, but you're only one small person. Stay with us. Don't go near the place. Please.

ANTIGONE *stands up, faintly smiling. She goes over to the door, and there, on the threshold, speaks.*

ANTIGONE (*quietly*). It's too late. This morning, when you saw me, I'd just come back from there.

Exit ANTIGONE. ISMENE *runs after her.*

ISMENE. Antigone!

As soon as ISMENE *disappears,* CREON *and his* PAGE *enter through another door.*

CREON. A guard, you say? One of the sentries keeping watch over the body? Have him brought in.

The GUARD *enters. A rough diamond. At present he is green with fear.*

JONAS . (*coming to attention*). Jonas, your honour. B Company.

CREON. Well?

JONAS. Well, sir, we drew lots to see who was to come, and it turned out to be me. We thought it was best for just one of us to come and explain. We couldn't all come. There's three of us on duty, sir, guarding the body.

CREON. Well, what have you got to tell me?

JONAS. I'm not the only one, you see. There's Snout as well, and Lance-Corporal Binns.

CREON. Why didn't he come?

JONAS. Just what I said! It ought to have been him. When there isn't an NCO, the Lance-Corp's responsible. But the others both said no, we must draw lots. Shall I go and fetch the Lance-Corp, sir?

CREON. No. You'll do, since you're here.

JONAS. I've got a very good record, sir. Seventeen years service. Enlisted as a volunteer. One medal. Two mentions in dispatches. A stickler for the rules. Orders are sacred. The officers all say 'You can rely on Jonas.'

CREON. Right. Speak . . . What are you afraid of?

JONAS. By rights it ought to have been Binns, sir. I'm up for a stripe but I haven't got it yet . . . I was supposed to get it in June.

CREON. Will you stop babbling and say what you have to say! If anything's happened all three of you are responsible. Never mind who ought to have come.

JONAS. Right, sir . . . Well . . . it was the body . . . We did stay awake, you know! And ours was the two o'clock watch, the worst of the lot. You know what it's like,

your honour, when the night's nearly over – the weight
between your eyes, the ache at the back of your neck
. . . The shadows all shifting about . . . And the mist
rising . . . They picked the right moment, and no
mistake! There we were, chatting, stamping our feet to
keep warm – but we weren't asleep, sir . . . I guarantee
none of us shut our eyes for a second . . . It was much
too cold anyway. Well, all of a sudden I take a look at
-the body. It was only a couple of yards away, but I took
a look at it every so often all the same. Thorough, sir,
that's me. That's why all the officers say 'You can rely
on –' (CREON *interrupts him with a gesture. He suddenly
shouts out.*) I was the first to notice, sir! The others'll
tell you the same – it was me who raised the alarm.

CREON. What do you mean – alarm? What for?

JONAS. The body, sir. Someone had covered it up. Oh,
nothing much. They didn't have time with us there. Just
a sprinkling of earth . . . Enough to hide it from the
vultures.

CREON (*going over to him*). Are you sure it wasn't some
animal scratching up the soil nearby?

JONAS. No, sir! That's what we hoped at first, too. Some
animal. But no – the earth had been scattered over the
body deliberately, according to the rites. By someone
who knew what they were doing.

CREON. Who dared? Who was mad enough to flout my
orders? Did you find any footprints?

JONAS. No, sir. Only one, lighter than a bird would make.
A bit later on, further away, we found a spade, a little
old child's spade, all rusty. We didn't reckon a child
could have done it, but the Corp kept the spade as
evidence, just in case.

CREON (*pause*). A child . . . The opposition may be
crushed, but it's already working away underground.
Polynices' friends, with their gold all frozen in Thebes
. . . The leaders of the plebs, reeking of garlic, suddenly
in alliance with the princes...The priests, trying to
fish up something for themselves out of these murky
waters . . . A child . . . Yes, they must have thought
that would make it more touching, more pathetic. I can
just see them and their 'child' – a hired assassin, more
like, with his toy spade hidden under his coat. Unless
they talked a real child into doing it. What a bonus to
have innocence on their side! A genuine little white-
faced brat ready to spit down the barrel of my guns! My
hands stained with fresh young blood! (*He goes over to*
JONAS.) But they must have had accomplices. Perhaps
among my guards . . . Here, you –

JONAS. Sir, we did all we were supposed to do! Snout may
have sat down for half an hour because his feet hurt, but
I stayed standing up the whole time! The Corp'll back
me up, sir!

CREON. Who've you told about this?

JONAS. No one, sir. We drew lots right away and I came
straight here.

CREON. Now listen to me. Your watch is doubled. Send
the relief away when it comes. I don't want anyone else
but you three near that body. And not a word to
anyone! You and your mates are already guilty of
negligence and will be punished for that anyway – but if
you talk, and the rumour gets about that someone's
covered up Polynices' corpse, all three of you will die.

JONAS (*bawling out*). We haven't said a word, sir, I swear!
But . . . I've been here all this time, and perhaps by
now the others have said something to the next watch.

(*Getting more and more panic-stricken.*) Sir, I've got two kids! One of them's only a baby. You'll give evidence to the court-martial that I was here, won't you? Here, with you! I've got a witness! If anyone's blabbed it was the others, not me! I've got a witness!

CREON. Clear out. If no one finds out, you'll live.

JONAS *runs out.* CREON *remains silent a moment, then suddenly says to himself.*

CREON. A child . . .

He takes the PAGE *by the shoulder.*

CREON. Come, boy. We must go and make this known . . . And then the trouble will start . . . Would you die for me? Would you go along with your little spade?

The PAGE *stares at him.* CREON *strokes the boy's hair as they go out.*

Yes, of course you would, without a moment's hesitation. You too. (*He can be heard sighing as he goes.*) A child . . .

They are gone. Enter the CHORUS.

CHORUS. So. Now the spring is wound. The tale will unfold all of itself. That's the convenient thing about tragedy – you can start it off with a flick of the finger: a glance at a girl going past with uplifted arms in the street; a sudden hunger for fame when you wake up one day – as if it were something to eat; asking yourself one question too many some evening . . . That's all it takes. And afterwards, no need to do anything. It does itself. Like clockwork set going since the beginning of time.

Death, treachery, despair – all there ready and waiting . . . And noise, and storms, and every kind of silence. The silence when the executioner lifts his arm at the end. The silence at the beginning, when the two lovers are naked together for the first time, and at first, in the dark, don't dare to move. The silence when the shouts of the crowd rise up around the victor – like a film with the sound-track stuck . . . all those open mouths with nothing coming out of them, all that clamour no more than an image. And the victor already vanquished, there in the midst of his silence.

Nice and neat, tragedy. Restful, too. In a drama, with its traitors, its desperate villains, its innocent victims, avengers, devoted followers and glimmers of hope, death becomes something terrible, a kind of accident. You might have arrived in time with the police. But tragedy's so peaceful! For one thing, everybody's on a par. All innocent! It doesn't matter if one person kills and the other is killed – it's just a matter of casting . . . And above all, tragedy's restful, because you know there's no lousy hope left. You know you're caught, caught at last like a rat in a trap, with all heaven against you. And the only thing left to do is shout – not moan, or complain, but yell out at the top of your voice whatever it was you had to say. What you've never said before. What perhaps you didn't even know till now . . . And to no purpose – just so as to tell it to yourself . . . to learn it, yourself. In drama you struggle, because you hope you're going to survive. It's utilitarian – sordid. But tragedy is gratuitous. Pointless, irremediable. Fit for a king!

Enter ANTIGONE, *hustled in by* GUARDS.

Now it's beginning. Little Antigone has been caught – and handcuffed. She can be herself at last.

Exit CHORUS *as the* GUARDS *push* ANTIGONE *on to the stage.*

JONAS (*quite self-assured again*). Come on now, miss – no
nonsense! You can explain it all to the boss. I only obey
orders. I don't want to know what you were doing.
Everybody has some excuse. Everybody has something
to say for himself. A fine pickle we'd be in if we had to
try to understand them all! Hold on tight, the rest of
you! She's a slippery customer! Fat lot I care what she
has to say!

ANTIGONE. Tell them to take their filthy hands off.
They're hurting me.

JONAS. Filthy hands? You might at least be polite, miss. I
am.

ANTIGONE. Tell them to let go of me. I am Oedipus's
daughter – Antigone. I shan't run away.

JONAS. Oedipus's daughter, eh? The tarts we pick up on
the beat always tell us to watch out because they're the
police chief's girlfriends!

GUARDS *laugh*.

ANTIGONE. I don't care about dying – but I won't have
them touch me!

JONAS. Oh? But you're not afraid of touching earth, or
corpses? You talk about dirty hands – what about your
own. (ANTIGONE *looks at her hands, in their handcuffs,
and smiles. They are covered with earth*.) They took
away your spade, so the second time you did it with
your bare hands! The cheek! I turn my back for a
minute to get a chew of tobacco, and before I can stick
it in my gob and say thanks, there she is clawing up the
earth with her nails like a blooming hyena! And in
broad daylight! And the fight she puts up when I try to
arrest her! Tries to scratch my eyes out! Shouts and

bawls about having to finish the job. Potty, if you ask me.

BINNS. I arrested one just as barmy the other day – showing everyone her backside.

JONAS. Anyway, we'll have a good party to celebrate this. Any ideas, Binns?

BINNS. The Crown. Best vino in town.

SNOUT. We're off duty Sunday. Shall we take the wives?

JONAS. No, it's more fun on our own – the women always complicate things and the kids keep wanting to go to the lav. (*Pause.*) Didn't think we'd be planning celebrations a while ago, did we?

BINNS. Perhaps there'll be a reward.

JONAS. If it's something really important . . .

SNOUT. Chap in C Company got double pay last month for catching an arsonist.

BINNS. If we get that let's go to the Arab Palace!

JONAS. Are you crazy? The wine's twice the price there. If you mean for the girls though, okay. (*Pause.*) Tell you what, why don't we go to the Crown first and get a skinful, then go on to the Palace? Hey, Binns – remember the fat one?

BINNS. You really did get blotto that time!

SNOUT. But if we get double pay the wives'll find out. There might be a public ceremony.

JONAS. Let's wait and see, then. We can go on the spree whatever happens. But if there's a special parade the wives and kids'll be there and the whole lot'll have to go to the Crown.

BINNS. We'll have to order in advance.

ANTIGONE (*small voice*). I'd like to sit down, please.

Pause.

JONAS. All right. Give her a chair. But don't let go of her!

Enter CREON.

JONAS (*loudly and at once*). Attenshun everybody!

CREON (*stopping, surprised*). What's this? Let go of that young lady at once! What do you think you're doing?

JONAS. We're the guard, sir, I brought my mates.

CREON. Who's watching the body, then?

JONAS. We sent for the relief.

CREON. I told you not to send them away! I told you not to tell anyone!

JONAS. We haven't, sir. But when we arrested this girl we thought we'd better bring her along. We didn't draw lots this time. We thought it was best if we all came.

CREON. Fools! (*To* ANTIGONE.) Where were you when they arrested you, Antigone?

JONAS. Right by the body, sir.

CREON. What were you doing there? You knew I'd forbidden anyone to go near it.

JONAS. You want to know what she was doing? That's why we brought her here. She was scrabbling in the earth with her hands. Covering it up again.

CREON. Do you realise what you're saying, man?

JONAS. Ask the others, sir, if you don't believe me. When I got back on duty after seeing you the first time, we uncovered the body, took the earth away. But the sun was getting hot and it was starting to smell, so we went and stood a little way away, on a mound, in the wind. We thought that'd be perfectly safe, in the daytime. To make sure, we decided one of us would keep an eye on the body all the time. But my midday, what with the heat right out there in the sun . . . And the wind had dropped, so the smell was worse . . . Well, it just knocked you out! No matter how hard I strained my eyes everything shook like a jelly – you couldn't see properly at all. I just went and asked one of my mates for a quid of tobacco to keep me awake . . . and before I have time to say thank you and turn round, there she is, grabbing away with her bare hands. In broad daylight!

She must have known we'd be bound to see her. And when I came running, do you think she stopped or tried to run off? Not a bit of it! She just scrabbled away as fast as she could, still, as if she hadn't even seen me. Even when I grabbed her she fought like a tiger and kept on trying to dig. Kept yelling at me to let her go, the body wasn't properly covered up yet . . .

CREON. Is this true, Antigone?

ANTIGONE. Yes.

JONAS. We went ahead and uncovered the body again, handed over to the next watch without saying anything, and brought here here to you, sir.

CREON. And during the night, Antigone? . . . the first time? . . . was that you too?

ANTIGONE. Yes. I used the little tin spade we used to make sandcastles with on the beach in the summer. It belonged to Polynices – he'd scratched his name on the handle. That's why I left it near him. But they took it away. So the second time I had to use my hands.

JONAS. Just like a little animal! In fact, with the air so

hazy, that's what one of my mates took her for at first. 'It's some animal,' he says, but I say, 'No it's not – it's too neat for an animal . . . It's a girl!'

CREON. Right. You may be asked for a report later . . . For the moment, leave your prisoner alone with me. Take off her handcuffs before you go. (*To* PAGE.) Take these men away, boy, and see they're kept incommunicado till I come.

Exit GUARDS, *following the* PAGE.

CREON. Did you tell anyone what you were going to do?

ANTIGONE. No.

CREON. Did you meet anyone on the way?

ANTIGONE. No.

CREON. Are you sure?

ANTIGONE. Yes.

CREON. Listen, then. Go back to your room, go to bed, and say you're ill and haven't been out since yesterday. Get your nurse to say the same. I'll get rid of those three men.

ANTIGONE. What's the point? They know I'll do it again.

Silence. They look at each other.

CREON. Why did you try to bury your brother?

ANTIGONE. I had to.

CREON. I'd forbidden it.

ANTIGONE (*quietly*). I had to just the same. People who aren't buried wander for ever in search of rest. If my brother had come home tired after a day's hunting I'd have taken off his boots, given him something to eat and got his bed ready. Polynices has done with hunting now. He's going home, to where Mother and Father, and Eteocles too, are waiting for him. He's entitled to some rest.

CREON. He was a rebel and a traitor and you know it.

ANTIGONE. He was my brother.

CREON. You heard my edict proclaimed at every cross-roads? You saw the posters on every wall?

ANTIGONE. Yes.

CREON. So you knew what was to become of anyone who dared give him burial?

ANTIGONE. Yes.

CREON. Maybe you thought that as the daughter of Oedipus, of Oedipus's pride, you were above the law?

ANTIGONE. No. I didn't think that.

CREON. The law is meant especially for you, Antigone – it's meant especially for the daughters of kings!

ANTIGONE. If I'd been a servant girl up to the elbows in dishwater when I heard the edict, I'd have dried my hands and gone out in my apron to bury my brother.

CREON. No, you wouldn't. If you'd been a servant girl you'd have known you'd die for it – so you'd have stayed at home and mourned your brother there. But you thought that because you belonged to the royal family – because you were my niece and my son's fiancé – I wouldn't dare have you put to death whatever you did.

ANTIGONE. You're wrong. I was sure you would have put me to death.

> CREON *looks at her, then bursts out suddenly, as if to himself.*

CREON. The pride of Oedipus. You're its living image.

And now I see it again in your eyes, I believe you. You thought I would have you put to death, and that struck you, in your vanity, as a very suitable end for you. For your father, too, ordinary human misery – there was no question of happiness! – wasn't enough. In your family, what's human only cramps your style – you have to have a private confrontation with destiny and death. You have to kill your father and sleep with your mother, and then find out about it later on, and drink it all in word by word. Some drink, eh, the words of doom? And how greedily you swig them down if your name's Oedipus – or Antigone. The next thing to do, of course, is to put your own eyes out and trail around with your children, begging. Well, all that's over and done with – times have changed in Thebes. What Thebes needs now is an ordinary king with no fuss. My name's only Creon, thank God. I've got both feet on the ground and both hands in my pockets. I'm not so ambitious as your father was, and all I aim at now I'm king is to try to see the world's a bit more sensibly run. There's nothing very heroic about it – just an everyday job, and, like the rest of them, not always very amusing. But since that's what I'm here for, that's what I'm going to do. And if some scruffy messenger comes down from the mountains tomorrow and tells me he's none too sure about my parentage, I'll just send him packing. I shan't go comparing dates and looking askance at my aunt. Kings have other things to do besides souping up their own woes. (*Goes over and takes her by the arm.*) Now listen carefully. You may be Antigone, Oedipus's daughter – but you're only twenty. It isn't long since all this would have been sorted out with bread and water and a box on the ears. (*Smiling.*) Have you put to death! You can't have looked at yourself in the glass, you little sparrow! You're too thin. You want to fatten yourself up a bit and give Haemon a nice sturdy son! You'd do Thebes more good that way than by dying, believe me. Now you go straight back to your room, do as I told you and say nothing. I'll see everyone else keeps quiet. Go along. And don't glare like that. You think I'm a brute, of course, and horribly unpoetic. But, handful that you are, I'm fond of you. Don't forget it was I gave you your first doll, and not very long ago either!

ANTIGONE *doesn't answer. She makes as if to leave.* CREON *stops her.*

Antigone! That's not the way to your room. Where are you going?

ANTIGONE (*stopping, and answering him quietly, without bravado*). You know very well.

Silence. Again they stand looking at each other.

CREON (*low, as if to himself*). What are you playing at?

ANTIGONE. I'm not playing.

CREON. Don't you realise that if anyone other than those three louts gets to know what you've tried to do, I shall have to have you killed? If you'll only keep quiet now and give up this foolishness there's a chance I may be able to save you. But in five minutes' time it will be too late. Do you understand?

ANTIGONE. They have uncovered my brother's body. I must go and bury him.

CREON. You really would make that senseless gesture a third time? There's another set of guards watching over Polynices' body now, and you know very well that even if you did manage to cover it up they'd only uncover it again. What else can you do but scrape more skin off your fingers and get yourself caught again?

ANTIGONE. Nothing else. But at least I can do that. And one must do what one can.

CREON. Do you really believe in this burial business? Is your brother's ghost really doomed to wander for ever if a handful of earth isn't thrown on the corpse accompanied by some ecclesiastical rigmarole? Have you ever heard the priests of Thebes at it? Ever seen them scrambling through it like overworked clerks, gabbling the words, skimping the movements, getting the deceased out of the way as fast as they can so they can botch another one before lunch?

ANTIGONE. Yes, I've seen them.

CREON. And haven't you ever thought that if it was someone you really loved lying there in that box, you'd let out a shriek and tell them to shut up and go away?

ANTIGONE. Yes. I've thought that.

CREON. Yet now you risk death because I've denied your brother that piffling passport, that mass-produced mumbo-jumbo you'd have been the first to be shamed and hurt by if it had actually been performed. It's ridiculous.

ANTIGONE. Yes. Ridiculous.

CREON. Why are you acting like this, then? To impress other people, those who do believe in it? To set them against me?

ANTIGONE. No.

CREON. Not for other people? And not for your brother himself? For whom, then?

ANTIGONE. No one. Myself.

CREON (*looks at her in silence*). You really want to die then? You look like a little hare, caught already.

ANTIGONE. Don't feel sorry for me. Be like me – do what you have to do. But if you want to be humane, do it quickly – that's all I ask. I can't be brave for ever.

CREON (*moving closer*). I want to save you, Antigone.

ANTIGONE. You're the king – you can do anything . . . But not that.

CREON. You think not?

ANTIGONE. You can't save me, and you can't force me to do what you want.

CREON. Proud Antigone! Pocket Oedipus!

ANTIGONE. All you can do is have me put to death.

CREON. And what if I have you tortured?

ANTIGONE. What for? To make me cry and beg for mercy? To make me swear to anything, and then do the same thing all over again when the pain stops?

CREON (*gripping her arm*). Now just listen. All right – I've got the villain's part and you're cast as the heroine. You're well aware of that. But don't try to push it too far, you little nuisance. If I were just an ordinary brute of a tyrant you'd have had your tongue torn out long ago, or been taken apart with red-hot pincers, or thrown into a dungeon. But you can see something in my eyes that hesitates. You can see I let you speak instead of sending for my soldiers. So you taunt and defy me to the top of your bent. What are you after, you little Fury?

ANTIGONE. Let go. You're hurting my arm.

CREON (*gripping more tightly*). No – I'm the strong one now. It's my turn to take advantage.

ANTIGONE. Ow!

CREON (*a twinkle in his eye*). Perhaps that's the answer! Perhaps I ought just to twist your wrist and pull your hair, as boys do when they play with the girls. (*He looks at her. Serious again. Close.*) I may be your uncle, but we're rather severe on each other in our family. So doesn't it strike you as strange – I, a king, set at naught by you yet listening patiently . . . an old man who's all-powerful, who's seen plenty of other people killed, just as appealing as you – and here am I taking all this trouble to try and keep you from dying?

Pause.

ANTIGONE. You're twisting too hard now. It doesn't even hurt. I just can't feel my arm.

CREON *looks at her and lets go of her, smiling.*

CREON (*low*). Heaven knows I've got other demands on my time today, but I'm going to spend however long it takes to save you, you little pest.

He makes her sit on a chair in the middle of the room, then takes off his jacket and advances on her in his shirtsleeves, heavy, powerful.

There are plenty of urgent matters to attend to after a failed revolution, you know. But they can wait. I don't want you to die mixed up in a political scandal. You deserve better than that. Because it is only a political scandal, you know – this brother of yours, this forlorn ghost, this body decomposing as the guards watch over it . . . All this pathos you get so worked up about. I may not be soft, but I am particular – I like things to be clean, neat, wholesome. Don't you think I'm as revolted as you are by that flesh rotting in the sun? You can smell it in the palace already, at night when the wind blows from the sea. It makes me feel quite sick. But I shan't even shut my window. The whole business is not only horrible, but also – between ourselves – abysmally stupid. But it's necessary that Thebes should smell the body for a while. I myself would have preferred to have your brother buried, just for reasons of hygiene. But to make those clods I govern understand what's what, the city has to stink of Polynices' corpse for a month.

ANTIGONE. You're loathsome.

CREON. Yes, child. It's my job. Whether that job should or shouldn't be done is a matter for discussion. But if it is done, it has to be done like this.

ANTIGONE. Why do you have to do it?

CREON. One morning I woke up King of Thebes. Though heaven knows there were things in life I loved better than power.

ANTIGONE. Then you should have said no!

CREON. I might have. But suddenly I felt like a workman refusing a job. It didn't seem right. I said yes.

ANTIGONE. That's your look-out. I didn't say yes! What do I care about your politics and what you 'have' to do and all your paltry affairs! I can still say no to anything I don't like, and I alone am the judge. You, with your crown and your guards and your paraphernalia – all you can do, because you said yes, is have me put to death.

CREON. Listen –

ANTIGONE. I needn't if I don't want to. There's nothing more you can tell me. But you drink in every word I say. If you don't summon your guards it's because you want to hear me out.

CREON. Huh!

ANTIGONE. You're not amused – you're afraid. That's why

you're trying to save me. It would suit you best to keep me here in the palace, alive but silent. You're too sensitive to be a tyrant. But just the same, as you know very well, you're going to have me put to death presently. And that's why you're afraid. Not a pretty sight, a man who's afraid.

CREON (*dully*). All right – I am afraid. Afraid you won't change your mind and I'll have to have you killed. And I don't want to.

ANTIGONE. I don't have to do what I don't want to! Perhaps you'd rather not have refused my brother a grave either? . . . Well?

CREON. I've told you already.

ANTIGONE. But you did it just the same! And now, though you'd rather not, you're going to have me put to death. Is that what it means to be a king?

CREON. Yes!

ANTIGONE. Poor Creon. And I, with my broken nails, and the bruises your guards have made on my arms, and my stomach all knotted up with fear – I'm a queen.

CREON. Have pity on me, then, and live. Your brother's body rotting under my windows is a high enough price to pay for law and order. My son loves you. I've paid enough. Don't force me to pay with you too.

ANTIGONE. No. You said yes. You'll never stop paying!

CREON (*suddenly shaking her, beside himself*). For God's sake! Try to understand for a minute, you little fool! I've tried hard enough to understand you! Someone has to say yes. Someone has to steer the ship. It's letting in water on all sides. It's full of crime and stupidity and suffering. The rudder's adrift. The crew won't obey orders – all they're interested in is looting the cargo. The officers are busy building a comfortable raft for themselves and cornering all the fresh water. But the mast's split, the wind's howling, the sails will soon be in shreds, and the whole lot of them will die together because they think of nothing but their own skins and their own petty concerns. And do you really think this is the moment for fine distinctions? Do you think there's time to debate whether you say yes or no, to wonder whether some day the price isn't going to be too high, whether afterwards you're going to be able to call yourself a man again? No! You grab the tiller, you stand up to the mountains of water, you shout an order – and if you're attacked you shoot the first comer. The first comer! He hasn't got a name. He's like the wave that's just broken over the deck, like the wind tearing at your limbs. He may be the man who smiled at you and gave you a light yesterday. He hasn't got a name any more. And neither have you, as you hang on desperately to the tiller. The only things that have got a name now are the ship and the storm. Do you understand?

ANTIGONE (*shaking her head*). I don't want to. It's all very well for you, but I'm not here to understand. I'm here to say no to you, and to die.

CREON. It's easy to say no!

ANTIGONE. Not always.

CREON. To say yes you have to sweat, roll up your sleeves, grab hold of life, plunge in up to the neck. It's easy to say no, even if it means dying. All you have to do is keep still and wait. Wait to live. Wait to die, even. It's feeble! – something human beings have thought up for themselves. Can you imagine a world where trees have said no to the sap? Where the animals have said no to the instincts of hunting and love? Brute beasts at least are good and natural and tough. They all jostle each other bravely along the same path. If any fall, others trample them. No matter how many die there'll always be one of every species left to reproduce and follow the same path with the same courage.

ANTIGONE. What a dream for a king! To be like an animal! Wouldn't that make life easy!

Pause. CREON *looks at her.*

CREON. You despise me, don't you? (*She doesn't answer. He goes on as if to himself.*) Funny. I've often imagined having this conversation . . . with a pale young man who's tried to kill me . . . from whom I can extract nothing but scorn. But I never thought it would be with you, Antigone, and over something so foolish . . . (*He buries his head in his hands. We realise he is at the end of his tether.*) Listen to me for the last time. I'm cast as the villain, and I'm going to have you put to death. But before I do I want you to be sure of your role. Do you know why you're going to die, Antigone? Do you realise what a squalid story it is you're going to put your poor little bloodstained name to – for ever?

Pause.

ANTIGONE. What do you mean?

CREON. The story of your brothers, Eteocles and Polynices. You think you know it, but you don't. No one in Thebes knows except me. But I think that this morning you too have the right to know. (*He meditates for a moment, his head in his hands, his elbows resting on his knees. As if to himself.*) It's not pretty. (*Dully, not looking at* ANTIGONE.) To start with, what do you remember about your brothers? You probably remember two boys who looked down on you and wouldn't let you play with them . . . who broke your dolls and were always whispering secrets together to make you jealous . . . ?

ANTIGONE. They were older than I was . . .

CREON. Later on, I suppose, you were impressed by their first cigarettes and their first long trousers. Then they started to go out in the evenings, to act like men, not to take any notice of you . . . ?

ANTIGONE. I was only a girl . . .

CREON. You saw your mother weep, your father get angry. You heard your brothers slam the door when they came home, and guffaw all along the corridors. They'd lurk past making feeble jokes and reeking of wine . . .

ANTIGONE. Once I hid behind the door. We'd just got up, and they'd just come home. Polynices saw me. He was pale, with shining eyes – so handsome in his evening clothes! He gave me a big paper flower he'd brought home with him from the party.

CREON. And you kept it, didn't you? And last night, before you went out, you opened the drawer and looked at it, to help you summon up your courage?

ANTIGONE (*with a start*). Who told you?

CREON. Poor Antigone! You and your paper flower! Do you know what your brother was really like?

ANTIGONE. I knew you'd say horrible things about him!

CREON. A brainless roisterer, a cruel, soulless little thug whose only distinction was driving faster than his cronies and spending more money in bars! I was there once when your father refused to pay his gambling debts. He turned pale, let out an oath, clenched his fist –

ANTIGONE. I don't believe it!

CREON. And drove his loutish paw right in your father's face! It was pitiful. Your father just sat at his desk with his face in his hands, his nose streaming with blood. Weeping. And Polynices stood sneering in a corner, lighting a cigarette.

ANTIGONE (*almost imploring now*). It isn't true!

CREON. You were only twelve at the time. You didn't see him for years after that. Did you?

ANTIGONE (*dully*). No.

CREON. He went away after the quarrel. Your father wouldn't bring any charges. Polynices joined the Argive army. As soon as he did they started to hunt your father down – an old man who wouldn't conveniently die and hand over his crown. There was one murder attempt after another, and whenever we caught the assassins they ended up confessing they were in the pay of Polynices. But it wasn't only him. I want you to know all the ins and outs, all the plots that were cooked up, all the machinations behind the drama you're so eager to play a part in. Yesterday I gave Eteocles an elaborate funeral. Thebes regards him now as a saint and a hero. The whole population was there. The schoolchildren pooled their pocket-money to buy wreathes. Old men pretended to be overcome with emotion and made quavering speeches in praise of the virtuous prince, the loyal brother, Oedipus's dutiful son. I made a speech too. And all the priests of Thebes were there, putting on suitable expressions. Eteocles was given military honours. I had no choice – I couldn't afford to have a scoundrel in both camps!

But now I'm going to tell you something . . . something terrible . . . that no one else knows but me.

Eteocles, that paragon of virtue, was no better than Polynices. The dutiful son had tried to murder his father, too. The loyal prince, too, was ready to sell Thebes to the highest bidder. I have proof that Eteocles was prepared to commit the same treachery as that for which Polynices' body now lies mouldering in the sun – Eteocles, sleeping peacefully in his marble tomb. It was a mere chance that Polynices pulled it off first. They were just two common crooks, cheating one another at the same time as they cheated us, cutting one another's throats like a couple of second-rate gangsters settling scores.

But it was necessary for me to make a hero of one of them. So I had my men seek out their bodies. They found them in one another's arms – for the first time in their lives, probably. They'd run one another through, then the Argive cavalry had ridden over the bodies and made mincemeat of them. They were both unrecognisable, Antigone. I gave orders for whichever corpse was least damaged to be scraped together for my national obsequies. And for the other to be left to rot. I don't even know which was which. And I assure you I don't care.

Long pause. They don't speak, or look at each other.

ANTIGONE (*quietly*). Why have you told me all this?

CREON *gets up, puts on his jacket.*

CREON. Would it have been better to let you die as part of it?

ANTIGONE. Perhaps. I believed in it.

Pause. CREON *goes over to her.*

CREON. What are you going to do now?

ANTIGONE (*getting up, like a sleepwalker*). Go to my room.

CREON. Don't stay on your own. Go and see Haemon. Get married as soon as you can.

ANTIGONE (*intake of breath*). Yes.

CREON. You've got your whole life before you. All this talk's beside the point. You still have a future.

ANTIGONE. Yes.

CREON. Nothing else matters. And you were going to waste that treasure! I can understand – I'd have done the same when I was twenty. That's why I listened to you so closely. I could hear the distant echo of a young Creon as thin and pale as you, dreaming, like you, of sacrificing everything . . . Get married quickly, Antigone, and be happy. Life's not what you think. It's like water – the young let it slip through their fingers without thinking. Shut your hands, Antigone, shut them tight and hold it back. You'll see – it'll turn into something small and hard that you can sit and munch in the sun. People will tell you different, because they need your energy and strength. Don't listen. Don't listen to me when I make my next speech over Eteocles' grave. It won't be the truth. Nothing is true but what is never said. You'll find that out for yourself . . . when it's too late.

Life's a book you enjoy, a child playing round your feet, a tool that fits into your hand, a bench outside your house to rest on in the evening. (*Pause.*) You'll despise me more than ever for saying this, but finding it out, as you'll see, is some sort of consolation for growing old: life is probably nothing other than happiness.

ANTIGONE (*a murmur, staring into space*). Happiness . . .

CREON (*suddenly rather ashamed*). Just a word, eh?

ANTIGONE (*softly*). And what will my happiness be like? What kind of a happy woman will Antigone grow into? What base things will she have to do, day after day, in order to snatch her own little scrap of happiness? Tell me – who will she have to lie to? Smile at? Sell herself to? Who will she have to avert her eyes from, and leave to die?

CREON (*exasperated*). That's enough. You're crazy.

ANTIGONE. I won't be quiet! I want to know what I have to do to be happy! Now, right away, because now is when I have to choose. You say life's so wonderful. I want to know what I have to do to live.

CREON. Do you love Haemon?

ANTIGONE. I love a Haemon who's tough and young . . . A Haemon who's demanding and loyal, like me. But if that life of yours, that happiness of yours, are going to pass over him and erode him – if he's not going to turn pale any more when I turn pale – if he won't think I must be dead if I'm five minutes late – if he doesn't feel alone in the world and hate me if I laugh and he doesn't know why – if he's going to become just a conventional spouse and learn to say yes like the rest – then no, I don't love Haemon any more!

CREON. That'll do. You don't know what you're saying.

ANTIGONE. I know what I'm saying, all right! It's just that you don't understand. I'm speaking to you from too far away now – from a country you can't enter any more, with your wrinkles, your wisdom and your belly. (*Laughs.*) I suddenly see you as you were when you were fifteen! Helpless, but thinking you're important. All life has added are those furrows in your face, that fat around your waist!

CREON (*shaking her*). Will you shut up!

ANTIGONE. Why do you want to shut me up? Because you
know I'm right? Don't you think I can see it in your
eyes? You know I'm right, but you'll never admit it
because you're trying to defend that happiness of yours
– like a dog crouching over a bone.

CREON. Your happiness as well as mine, you fool!

ANTIGONE. You disgust me, all of you, you and your
happiness! And your life, that has to be loved at any
price. You're like dogs fawning on everyone they come
across. With just a little hope left every day – if you
don't expect too much. But I want everything, now!
And to the full! Or else I decline the offer, lock, stock
and barrel! I don't want to be sensible, and satisfied
with a scrap – if I behave myself! I want to be sure of
having everything, now, this very day, and it has to be
as wonderful as it was when I was little. Otherwise I
prefer to die.

CREON. There you go – just like your father!

ANTIGONE. Exactly! Neither of us ever stops asking
questions! Right up to the moment when there's not a
spark of hope left to stifle. We're the sort who jump
right on your precious, lousy hope!

CREON. If you could see how ugly you look, shouting!

ANTIGONE. Very vulgar, isn't it? Father was only beautiful
afterwards – when he knew for certain that he'd killed
his father and slept with his mother, and that nothing,
now, could save him. He grew suddenly silent. Smiled.
He was beautiful. It was all over. He had only to shut
his eyes not to see you any more – all you craven
candidates for happiness! It's you who are ugly, even
the handsomest of you! There's something ugly about

the corners of your eyes and mouths. You used the right
words for it just now, Creon, when you talked about
cooking up plots. You all look like cooks, with your fat
faces. Cooks! Scullions!

CREON (*twisting her arm*). I order you to be silent!

ANTIGONE. You order me, scullion? Do you imagine you
can give me orders?

CREON. The ante-room's full of people. They'll hear you.
Do you want to destroy yourself?

ANTIGONE. Open the door! Let them hear!

CREON (*putting his hand over her mouth*). Quiet, for God's
sake.

ANTIGONE (*struggling*). Quick! Quick, scullion! Call your
guards!

The door opens. Enter ISMENE.

ISMENE. Antigone!

ANTIGONE. You as well? What do you want with me,
then?

ISMENE. Creon! Creon! If you kill her, you'll have to kill
me too! (*To* ANTIGONE.) Forgive me, Antigone. But I
am brave now. I'll go with you.

ANTIGONE. Oh no! Not now! I'm on my own now. Don't
you think you can just muscle in and die with me now!
It'd be too easy!

ISMENE. But I don't want to live if you die! I don't want to
stay on without you!

ANTIGONE. You've chosen life. I've chosen death. Leave
me alone, you and your lamentations. What you ought
to have done was go this morning, on all fours, in the
dark . . . grub up the earth with your nails, under the
noses of the guards . . . be grabbed by them like a thief.

That's what you ought to have done!

ISMENE. All right, Antigone – all right! I'll go tomorrow!

ANTIGONE. Hear that, Creon? Her too! And how do you know it won't spread to others when they hear me? What are you waiting for? Why don't you call your guards to silence me? Come on now, Creon, be brave – it won't take long! Come on, scullion! You have no choice – get it over with!

CREON (*sudden shout*), Guards!

The GUARDS *appear immediately.*

Take her away!

ANTIGONE (*crying out: relieved*). At last, Creon! At last!

BINNS (*roughly*). Come on! This way!

The GUARDS *seize her and take her off.* ISMENE *follows, crying out.*

ISMENE. Antigone! Antigone!

Enter CHORUS.

CHORUS. You're mad, Creon. What have you done?

CREON (*staring ahead of him*). She had to die.

CHORUS. Don't let her die, Creon! We'll all bear the scar for thousands of years!

CREON. It was her choice. She wanted to die! None of us was strong enough to persuade her to live. I understand now. She was born to die. She may not have known it herself, but Polynices was only an excuse. And when that excuse wouldn't work any more she chose another. All that mattered to her was to refuse everything and to die.

CHORUS. She's only a child, Creon.

CREON. What do you want me to do? Condemn her to live?

Enter HAEMON, *shouting.*

HAEMON. Father!

CREON (*hurrying over and embracing him*). Forget her, Haemon. Forget her, my boy!

HAEMON. You must be mad! Let go!

CREON (*holding on tighter*). I tried everything I could think of to save her. Everything, I swear. She doesn't love you – if she did she could have lived. She preferred her own folly, and death.

HAEMON (*struggling to escape*). But they're taking her away! Father! Tell the guards to bring her back!

CREON. She has spoken now. All Thebes knows what she's done. I must have her put to death.

HAEMON (*tearing himself free*). Let me go!

Pause. They stand facing one another.

CHORUS (*approaching*). Can't you think of something – say she's mad, have her shut up?

CREON. They'll say it isn't true. That I'm sparing her because she was going to marry my son. I can't.

CHORUS. Can't you try to gain time, and have her escape, tomorrow?

CREON. The mob knows already. They're all round the palace, yelling. I can't turn back.

HAEMON. The mob! What does it matter? You're the master!

CREON. Under the law. Not against it.

HAEMON. But I'm your son – you can't let them take her away from me!

CREON. Yes, my boy – I can. Come now – courage! Antigone can't go on living. She's already left us.

HAEMON. And do you think I can go on living, without her? Do you think I'm going to accept that life you talk about? Every day, morn till night, without her? All your bustle and blather, all your emptiness . . . without her?

CREON. You'll have to. To every man there comes a day, soon or late, sad or happy, when at last he has to accept that he's a man. For you that day's today. For the last time you stand in front of me as my little son . . . your eyes brimming, pain in your heart. In a moment, when you turn away and go through that door, it will be over.

HAEMON (*drawing back; low*). It's over already.

CREON. Don't judge me, Haemon. Don't you judge me too.

HAEMON (*looking at him, then in a sudden outburst*). That great strength and courage . . . that giant-god who used to gather me up in his arms and save me from ghosts – was that you? The thrilling smell, the delicious bread in the lamplight, the evenings when you used to take me into your study and show me your books – was that really you, do you think?

CREON (*humbly*). Yes.

HAEMON. And all that trouble, that pride, those books – were they only leading up to this? To becoming a man, as you call it – a man who's supposed to consider himself lucky just to be alive?

CREON. Yes.

HAEMON (*crying out like a child, throwing himself into* CREON'*s arms*). Oh, Father, it isn't true, it isn't you, it isn't happening! We're not both driven into a corner where we can only say yes! You're still strong, like when I was small. I beg you, let me admire you still! I'm too alone, the world's too empty, if I have to stop looking up to you.

CREON (*putting him away*). We are alone. The world is empty. And you've looked up to your father too long. Look me straight in the eyes. That's what it means to be a man.

HAEMON (*looks at him, then recoils, and bursts out*). Antigone! Antigone! Help!

HAEMON *runs out.*

CHORUS (*going over to* CREON). Creon, he's like a madman.

CREON (*standing motionless, staring into space*). Yes. Poor boy. He loves her.

CHORUS. Creon, you must do something.

CREON. I can do nothing.

CHORUS. Haemon's wounded. Mortally.

CREON. We all are.

Enter ANTIGONE, *hustled in by the* GUARDS *who then put their backs against the door. The mob can be heard howling in the distance.*

JONAS. Sir, they've broken into the palace!

ANTIGONE. Creon . . . keep them away! I don't want to see their faces any more, or hear their shouting. I don't want to see anyone! You've got my death – that's enough. Don't let me have to see anyone else till it's all over.

CREON (*going: shouting to* GUARDS). Jonas, you stay here
with her! The rest of you, come with me and throw the
mob out!

The other two GUARDS *go out, followed by the* CHORUS.
ANTIGONE *is left with the first* GUARD. *She looks at
him.*

ANTIGONE. So it's to be you.

JONAS. What do you mean?

ANTIGONE. Yours is the last human face I shall see.

JONAS. Looks like it.

ANTIGONE. Let me look at you.

JONAS (*moving away; embarrassed*). No . . . no . . . stop
it . . .

ANTIGONE. Aren't you the one who arrested me just now?

JONAS. Yes.

ANTIGONE. You hurt me. There was no need. Did I look
as if I'd try to run away?

JONAS. Now then, no nonsense! It was either you or me.

ANTIGONE. How old are you?

  Pause.

JONAS. Thirty-nine.

ANTIGONE. Any children?

JONAS. Two.

ANTIGONE. Are you fond of them?

JONAS. Mind your own business.

*He starts pacing to and fro. For a while the only sound
is that of his footsteps.*

ANTIGONE (*more humbly*). Have you been in the guards long?

JONAS. Since the end of the war. I was a sergeant. I signed on again.

ANTIGONE. Do you have to be a sergeant to join the guards?

JONAS. In theory. A sergeant or a special. But if you're a sergeant you lose your rank when you join the guards. So if, for the sake of argument, I meet an army recruit, he might not salute me.

ANTIGONE. Really?

JONAS. Of course they generally do. They know you're really an NCO. As for the pay, you get ordinary guard's pay, plus, as a bonus for the first six months, the extra you used to get as a sergeant. But of course there are other advantages. Living quarters, heating, family allowances. All in all a married guard can earn more than a sergeant in the regular army.

ANTIGONE. Really?

JONAS. Yes. That's why there's such rivalry. As you may have noticed, sergeants pretend to look down on guards. Because of the promotion, mainly. They're right, in a way. It's much slower and more difficult in the guards. But you mustn't forget that a lance-sergeant in the guards is more important than a quarter-master-sergeant in the army . . .

ANTIGONE (*suddenly*). Listen.

JONAS. I'm listening.

ANTIGONE. I'm going to die very soon.

He doesn't answer. Pause. He goes on pacing. Then:

JONAS. Of course, people look up more to a guard. He's a
sort of official as well as a soldier . . .

ANTIGONE. Do you think it hurts?

JONAS. What?

ANTIGONE. Dying. Does it hurt?

JONAS. Couldn't say. I know it hurt during the war, when
men were wounded in the stomach. But I was never
wounded myself . . . Maybe that's what's stood in the
way of my promotion . . .

ANTIGONE. How will they do it?

JONAS. I believe I heard they were going to wall you up, so
as not to stain the city with your blood.

ANTIGONE. Wall me up? Alive?

JONAS. At first.

Silence. The GUARD *makes himself a quid of tobacco.*

ANTIGONE. Hail, then, my grave, my marriage bed, my
underground home! (*She looks very small in the middle
of that big base room. She looks cold. She wraps her
arms around herself. Then, as if to herself.*) But all on
my own . . . !

JONAS (*finishing his quid*). It'll be in the caves of Hades,
outside the city gates. Right out in the sun. Another
lousy job for whoever's on sentry duty. The last I heard
it was going to be the guards again. They put everything
on us!

ANTIGONE (*low, weary*). Two animals . . .

JONAS. What about them?

ANTIGONE. Two animals would huddle together for
warmth. I'm all on my own.

JONAS. I can call somebody if you need anything.

ANTIGONE. No. I'd just like you to deliver a letter after I'm dead.

JONAS. What letter?

ANTIGONE. I'm just going to write it.

JONAS. Oh no! None of that! Letter indeed! It'd be more than my life's worth . . .

ANTIGONE. I'd give you this ring.

JONAS. Is it gold?

ANTIGONE. Yes.

JONAS. If they search me I'll be courtmartialled. You realise that, don't you? Fat lot you care . . . (*Looks at the ring again.*) Tell you what I could do . . . I could write what you want to say down in my notebook and tear the page out. It wouldn't be the same if it was in my writing . . .

ANTIGONE (*eyes closed, with an attempt at a laugh*). Your writing . . . ! (*Then she shudders.*) Oh, it's all too horrible!

JONAS (*offended, pretending to give the ring back*). All right, if you've changed your mind. It's all the same to me.

ANTIGONE. No – keep the ring, and write down what I say . . . But quickly – there isn't much time. Put: 'My darling . . .'

JONAS (*he has got out his notebook and is sucking the lead of his pencil*). Is it for your boyfriend?

ANTIGONE. 'My darling. I've chosen to die. And perhaps you'll stop loving me . . .

  JONAS *mumbles the words after her as he writes.*

And Creon was right: it's awful, but here, with this man

beside me, I don't know any more what I'm dying for
. . . I'm afraid . . . (JONAS *mumbles some more.*) Oh,
Haemon! It's only now I realise how easy it was to
live . . .'

JONAS (*stops writing*). Hey, you're going much too fast! It
takes time, you know!

ANTIGONE. How far have you got?

JONAS (*reading what he's written*). '. . . here, with this
man beside me . . .'

ANTIGONE. 'I don't know any more what I'm dying
for . . .'

JONAS (*mumbling as he writes, then*). 'I don't know any
more what I'm dying for . . .' People never do know
what they're dying for . . .

ANTIGONE. 'I'm afraid . . .' (*She stops, straightens up.*)
No, cross all that out! It's better no one should ever
know. It'd be as if they were to see me naked, touch
me, after I was dead. Just put, 'I'm sorry.'

JONAS. You mean cross out that last bit and put 'I'm sorry'
instead?

ANTIGONE. 'I'm sorry, my darling. It would have been nice
and peaceful for you all without me. I love you . . .'

JONAS *mumbles and writes as before. Pause.*

JONAS. Is that the lot?

ANTIGONE. Yes.

JONAS. Funny sort of a letter.

ANTIGONE. Yes. It is.

JONAS. And who's it for?

The door bursts open. The other GUARDS *enter.*

ANTIGONE *stands up, looks at them, then at* JONAS,
*now standing behind her. He pockets the ring and
puts away his notebook, self-important. He sees*
ANTIGONE'*s look, and starts to shout to keep himself
in countenance.*

JONAS. Come on, you! No nonsense!

Effort at a smile from ANTIGONE. *Then she bows her
head and goes over without a word to the other*
GUARDS. *They all go out. Enter* CHORUS, *suddenly.*

CHORUS. So. It's all over for Antigone. Soon it will be
Creon's turn. Everyone's turn will come in the end.

Door bursts open; enter MESSENGER.

MESSENGER (*shouting*). The queen! Where's the queen?

CHORUS. What do you want with her? What news do you
bring?

MESSENGER. Terrible news! They'd just put Antigone in
the cave. They hadn't finished rolling the last blocks of
stone into place when Creon and all those around him
heard cries suddenly issuing from the tomb. Everyone
stopped and listened: it wasn't Antigone's voice. They
all looked at Creon. And he was the first to guess. He
suddenly shrieked like a madman 'Take away the
stones! Take away the stones!' The slaves hurled
themselves on the heaped-up rocks, and the king fell on
them too, digging with his bare hands until they bled.
At last some of the rocks shifted and the thinnest person
there squeezed through the opening. Antigone was in
the depths of the cave, hanged with her own girdle. The
blue and green and red strands looked like a child's
necklace. And there was Haemon, on his knees,
groaning, holding her in his arms, his face buried in her
robe. They removed another rock, and Creon was able

to get through at last. You could see his grey hair in the darkness of the cave. He tried to raise Haemon up, implored him, but he wouldn't listen. Then suddenly Haemon stood up. Never had he looked so much like the boy he once was. He stared at his father, his eyes black with passion, then suddenly spat in his face and drew his sword. Creon leapt out of reach. Haemon looked at him, his youthful eyes full of contempt – a look Creon could not avoid, sharper than the sword itself. Haemon stared at the trembling old man, and without a word plunged the sword into his own belly. Then he lay down beside Antigone, embracing her in a vast red pool of blood.

Enter CREON, *with his* PAGE.

CREON. I have had them laid side by side at last. They are washed now; rested. Pale, but peaceful. Two lovers after their first night. For them it's over.

CHORUS. But not for you, Creon. You still have something to learn. The poor of Thebes will go cold this winter, Creon. When Eurydice, the queen, your wife, heard of her son's death she was knitting for the poor, as usual. She quietly finished her row and laid down her needles – calmly, as she did everything . . . perhaps even a little more calmly than usual. Then she went into her room, her lavender-scented room with all the little embroidered mats and plush frames – and she cut her throat. Now she lies on one of the old-fashioned twin beds, just where you saw her lying one night when she was a girl, wearing the same smile, only sadder. If it wasn't for the red on the draperies round her throat you might think she was sleeping.

Pause.

CREON. Her too. They are all asleep now. Good. It's been a hard day. (*Pause. Dully.*) It must be good to sleep.

CHORUS. You are all alone now, Creon.

CREON. Yes . . . (*Pause. He lays his hand on the* PAGE's *shoulder.*) Boy . . .

PAGE. Sir?

CREON. I'm going to tell you something the others don't know. There you are, face to face with what's to be done. You can't just fold your arms and do nothing. They say it's dirty work. But if you don't do it, who will?

PAGE. . . . I don't know, sir.

CREON. Of course you don't – you're lucky! And it's best never to find out. Are you looking forward to growing up?

PAGE. Oh yes!

CREON. You're mad, boy! It'd be best never to grow up, either. (*Clock strikes in the distance. He speaks as if to himself.*) Five o'clock. What've we got at five?

PAGE. Privy Council, sir.

CREON. In that case we'd better go. Come . . .

They go out. CREON *leaning on the* PAGE.

CHORUS (*coming forward*). So. Antigone was right – it would have been nice and peaceful for us all without her. But now it's over. It's nice and peaceful anyway. Everyone who had to die is dead: those who believed in one thing, those who believed in the opposite . . . even those who didn't believe in anything, but were caught up in the story without knowing what was going on. All dead: quite stiff, quite useless, quite rotten. And those who are still alive are quietly beginning to forget them and get their names mixed up. It's over. Antigone's quiet now, cured of a fever whose name we shall never know. Her work is done. A great, sad peace descends on Thebes, and on the empty palace where Creon will begin to wait for death. (*As he speaks, the* GUARDS *have entered, sat down on a bench with their caps pushed back and a bottle of wine within reach, and begun a game of cards.*) Only the guards are left. All that has happened is a matter of indifference to them. None of their business. They go on with their game of cards.

The curtain falls quickly as the GUARDS *slam down their trumps.*

Notes

2   *Prologue, Chorus*:   unlike in ancient Greek tragedy,
     the Chorus in Anouilh's version of *Antigone* is
     played by a single actor. It is customary in both
     French and English performance practice for the
     same actor also to play the role of Prologue, who
     bears this title in the original French text as well
     as in this English translation only when presenting
     this long introduction to the play. The role is not
     singled out anywhere else in either version, nor
     differentiated from the Chorus in Anouilh's list of
     personnages.

5   *Seven great foreign princes*:   the story of this
     conflict is the subject of Aeschylus's tragedy,
     Seven against Thebes.

11   *That's how the cast-list was drawn up*:   a typical
     Anouilh character's reference to being aware of
     performing, taking part in a play. It is given added
     poignancy in *Antigone* as the Prologue has stressed
     that certain characters know the fate that awaits
     them, so the action of the play is thus like a script
     which must run right through till the final curtain.

12   *ride in the tumbril*:   Anouilh's anachronisms are
     usually twentieth-century ones, sports cars,
     nightclubs, etc., but not invariably so. The vision
     that terrifies Ismene here would inevitably evoke
     the French Revolution for Anouilh's audiences.
     The tumbril (*tombereau*) was the farm cart used to
     take the condemned to the guillotine. The word
     used by Anouilh here is not in fact *tombereau* but
     charrette, also a mundane cart intentionally
     humiliating for aristocrats; however, Barbara
     Bray's preference for 'tumbril' makes the

association quite clear for readers and audiences
in the English-speaking world. At this point in his
edition of *Antigone* (p.49), Jacques Monférier
argues that Anouilh reveals his own *aristocratisme*
in giving as much emphasis to Ismene's horror of
the foul-smelling, spitting mob as to her fear of
death.

19   *dark and thin*:   Antigone is the archetypal Anouilh
heroine of the early plays: she is dark, small,
scrawny, physically undeveloped as a woman, and,
as we have already seen, regrets not being male.
She is just like the author's eponymous Eurydice
of the same period. In *Antigone* the archetype is
emphasised even more than in *Eurydice* by the
contrast with the blonde, beautiful, stereotypically
'feminine' Ismene.

20   *He is dumbfounded*:   Haemon's reaction is
understandable, but it could be argued that his
minimal responses – virtually no lines for an actor
to get his teeth into – and final acquiescence
make the role a difficult one to act at this stage;
from this point of view, the scene, which has no
equivalent in Sophocles, is not one of Anouilh's
most sensitively written.

21   *Let Polynices' harsh ghost wander*:   this is a rare
vestige of ancient religious feeling in Anouilh's
otherwise very secular twentieth-century universe.

21   *Exit* ANTIGONE. ISMENE *runs after her*:   W.D.
Howarth observes (*Anouilh: Antigone*) that
Antigone's shock revelation to Ismene can be
regarded as a coup de théâtre and would be used
as a 'curtain-line' in a play divided into acts.
Despite Anouilh's stage direction to Creon and
the page to enter 'as soon as Ismene disappears',
Howarth continues with an interesting production
idea: 'If Anouilh had followed a conventional
division into acts, this would have been the end of
Act One. As it is, it is the first occasion on which
the stage has been left empty between episodes,

without what in neo-classical dramaturgy is called "liaison de scènes"; and in the theatre, the director may well decide to emphasise the fact by a slightly longer pause before the next sequence begins.'

22   *Snout . . . Binns*:   translator Barbara Bray endeavours to catch the comic and the mundane combination of Anouilh's French names here, Boudousse and Durand. Jonas stays the same.

22   *Seventeen years service*:   in *Antigone* Anouilh caricatures the military mind in a way commonly found in French comic writing (and had experienced it himself during his war service in 1939–40). The guards are stupid, and alternately servile and full of bluster, keenly aware of rank and the importance of hierarchical procedures in the army. Above all they are willing to obey orders no matter how brutal; this is stressed at various points by Anouilh and is of significance in a play written when the Second World War had been raging on many fronts for a long time. As samples of general humanity, these guards can also be regarded as a pointer to Anouilh's misanthropy and lack of illusions about the common man. For leisure they dream of nothing more exalted than getting away from their wives and children to spend their bonus on drinking and wenching. It is no coincidence that the focus at the end of the play is on them as the curtain comes down: 'All that has happened is a matter of indifference to them.'

24   *their gold all frozen in Thebes*:   Creon's speculation about who could be behind the incident consists of a medley of allusions to political strife and destabilisation such as France and many other countries experienced in the years leading up to the Second World War. It is one of the most pointed anachronisms in the play.

25 *Yes, of course you would*: the significance of the
page's role as a symbolic moral reinforcement to
Antigone becomes clear at this stage. The page is
instinctively idealistic and potentially self-
sacrificing, Creon realises, precisely because he is
a *child* – hence the association with the little
spade, although Creon does not know at this stage
that it belongs to Antigone.

26 *Nice and neat, tragedy*: in this famous passage the
Chorus contrasts the inevitability of the outcome
in classical tragedy with the possibility of salvation
in more modern and popular artistic forms such
as melodramas and thrillers. In the latter the
victims are (of course) innocent and their
oppressors are villains, and there is always the
possibility that the police will turn up in the nick
of time, save the victim and arrest the villain. This
is of interest for our interpretation of the play,
where Anouilh carefully avoids a 'black and white'
distinction between villain and victim. He puts a
strongly argued political case for his 'tyrant'
Creon; Sophocles none at all for his, who is guilty
of pride and intolerance.

27 *the police chief's girlfriends!*: the claim to have
'pull' in high places used by people trying to
avoid arrest is a stock-in-trade incident in popular
cinema, the kind well known to Anouilh. The
claim can be exploited for suspense purposes (it
might not come off, but at least some time will
have been gained while the story is being
checked), or exploited comically at the expense of
officious guardians of public order who have egg
on their face when it turns out to be true. This
latter effect could be created if only for a second
or two in a production of this play when the
guards realise that the culprit's claim to be
Antigone is validated by Creon as soon as he sees
her.

27   *I won't have them touch me!*:   Antigone shares
      Ismene's physical horror of ordinary people (yet 'I
      don't care about dying'!). This should be born in
      mind by anyone tempted to interpret the heroine
      in the context of 1944 as a symbolic member of
      the French Resistance, a champion of Republican
      values against Creon's 'Vichyite Fascism', etc.

35   *some ecclesiastical rigmarole*:   Creon's cynical view
      of the priesthood and religious ritual, hammered
      home in a series of speeches, is not far removed
      from Anouilh's anticlerical position, which is
      shared by many leading French writers in the
      middle of the twentieth century. The atmosphere
      thus created contrasts strikingly with the spirit of
      Sophocles' tragedy, which is situated in a
      fundamentally religious universe.

39   *Someone has to steer the ship*:   this speech is one of
      those that caused Anouilh to be accused of being
      sympathetic to the Vichyite views of the right-wing
      politicians backing Marshal Pétain: collaboration
      with the German invaders was a regrettable
      necessity as there was really no alternative. The
      Third Republic was deemed by them to be
      shipwrecked, its public life and private morals
      undermined by decades of spineless parliamentary
      democracy, a corrupt press, the indiscreet
      behaviour of the traditional establishment, etc.

39   *The crew won't obey orders*:   according to the
      Vichyite view, ever since the triumph of the
      Popular Front parties in the 1936 elections,
      creating a left-wing government in France for the
      first time, the working classes were rebellious and
      undisciplined, concerned only to make unrealistic
      demands for improved wages and conditions.

40   *The officers are busy building*:   according to the
      same view (perhaps a bit more surprisingly for
      those unfamiliar with some of the paradoxes of
      right-wing ideology in France in the age of

Fascism), the traditional capitalist classes and old-style industrialists of the Third Republic were just as irresponsible. They were feathering their own nests with no thought of the consequences for the country as a whole as a result of the social tensions they were provoking. It has also been thought that this is a veiled reference to the 'Massilia' episode when a number of French parliamentarians sailed away to Algeria on a ship of that name rather than accept the downfall of the French Republic in 1940.

15   *You'll despise me more than ever*: and worse, Antigone will rebel, and this time irrevocably. This speech will prove to be a terrible tactical blunder on Creon's part. His cause is suddenly lost by 'a wholly human urge to make a genuine confession, and to show understanding and fellow-feeling' (Howarth, *Anouilh: Antigone*, p. 40).

46   *I love a Haemon*: in this key speech Antigone pours out her hatred of compromise, and particularly of accepting that the fires of youthful idealism – and of passionate love – do not burn fiercely for ever. She will thus refuse to live for fear that Haemon will become 'just a conventional spouse and learn to say yes like the rest'.

46   *I suddenly see you*: in the French text of the play at this point Antigone suddenly adopts the familiar *tu/te* forms of address when directing her vulgar insults at Creon during the remainder of this scene. The force of this change is inevitably lost in translation into English.

47   *You disgust me*: this is an identical line to that spat out by Thérèse, the heroine of *La Sauvage*, who is similarly unwilling to join the ranks of those who accept the moral compromises and disappointments of adult life.

47   *Exactly!*: Oedipus committed the folly, unpardonable in ancient Greece, of believing it

possible to defy the oracle. That the oracle's
prediction seemed preposterous – that he would
one day kill his father and marry his mother – was
no excuse in Greek society. For his arrogance,
hubris in classical morality and tragic theory, he
paid a heavy price. Antigone's triumphant
endorsement of her father's action makes it clear
to the audience that further argument will be
futile, but Creon will desperately struggle for a
few minutes yet.

47   *how ugly you look*:   a physical and aesthetic
response that is typical of Anouilh's characters at
moments of *moral* shock. A few minutes earlier,
when Antigone decried Creon's cynical 'realism',
she also objected to his accompanying *physical*
degeneration, as exemplified by his wrinkles and
increasing corpulence. (This is what Haemon
would be like in twenty years' time.)

48   *just muscle in and die with me*:   the egocentric
nature of Antigone's determination to do the right
thing by Polynices could not be made clearer than
by this reaction to Ismene's late but nonetheless
sincere conversion.

49   *Hear that, Creon? Her too!*:   by goading Creon,
Antigone ensures that her death-wish be fulfilled.
Her provocation of him is insincere, and contrived
purely to get herself executed, as she knows that
whatever sense of rebellion 'spreads to others' will
be misguidedly on behalf of a morally worthless
brother, and only she is party to this fact. It is
also of indifference to her that Ismene remains in
ignorance of it, and will be left to suffer.

49   *Polynices was only an excuse*:   Creon's lucid
assessment of Antigone's character and actions
could not define the difference between her and
Sophocles' heroine more starkly.

50   *Condemn her to live?*:   this too is a thoroughly
modern paradox, encapsulating the fate of a

Romantic heroine for whom life is unbearable
because imperfect.

50 *she could have lived*: a line for the audience to
recall when Antigone dictates her letter of adieu
to Haemon.

50 *Can't you think of something*: this and the
Chorus's next intervention as an anguished
participant in the play are slightly puzzling, as he
is normally a detached commentator who knows
that Antigone's tragic fate is sealed.

50 *Under the law. Not against it*: Anouilh goes
further than any twentieth-century moderniser of
Sophocles could in exonerating Creon. If the king
of Thebes adheres to a principle such as this one,
then it must be doubted that he can be
considered a tyrant at all.

52 *crying out like a child*: Haemon too fears the time
when to survive into adult life it will be necessary
to 'say yes', but has come to this realisation later
than Antigone, whom he now prepares to join in
death.

52 *Mortally*: the significance of this word appears to
be lost on Creon, who is presumably too affected
by what he has gone through with Antigone to see
this as a warning from the Chorus that Haemon's
life may also be in danger.

55 *people look up more to a guard*: this mini lecture
on the pros and cons of a career as an ordinary
soldier or as a guard – the latter has more prestige
but less chance of promotion – would remind
French audiences of the time-honoured rivalry
between parallel forces of order such as the police
and the gendarmerie. Jonas of course is interested
only in the pettiest features of that rivalry. It is
typical of Anouilh's feeling for pathos – and his
bleak worldview – that he should contrive
Antigone's last contact to be with an insensitive
individual whose only regret is that it will be hot

and tiring work to stand guard in the sun while a
prisoner is suffocating to death in a tomb. Jonas is
incapable of relating to Antigone as a human
being, and it is scenes like this, and not just the
tragic outcome, that place *Antigone* in the category
of 'Black Plays'.

57   *(mumbling as he writes, then)*:   the necessity of
repeating Antigone's dictation, an ingenious
invention by Anouilh, allows the stressing of an
important realisation by the heroine: that her
resolve has crumbled. She no longer knows why
she is forfeiting her life; she could and should
have agreed to live.

57   *cross all that out!*:   a revealing instruction from
Antigone and its follow-up diminishes her stature
as a youthful and heroic martyr to truth: 'It's
better no one should ever know'. The signature of
Anouilh is to be found in the next line, where the
exact balance of psychological and physical
repugnance felt by this young girl must be
appreciated: she will no more be known to have
made a foolish and fatal error of judgement about
life than be seen literally naked. The disturbing
ambivalence and moral confusion of these
concluding moments recall another famous French
theatre ending of the 1940s, that of Sartre's Hugo
Barine in *Les Mains sales* (see Commentary p.xlii).

57   *The door bursts open*:   so there is no time for
Jonas's question to be answered and we cannot be
certain the letter would have been delivered if
Haemon had not killed himself. Jonas still pockets
the ring however: a small detail but one that
intensifies the 'blackness' of the dramatic genre.

58   *Effort at a smile from Antigone*:   an attempt to
communicate warmth to Jonas in endorsement of
their collusion perhaps. Yet can she be confident
he will make an effort to find out who the letter

should be delivered to? An interesting dilemma for a director.

59   *she was knitting for the poor*:   so now we learn that the character described at the beginning by the Prologue as knitting was Queen Eurydice herself. Female characters in Anouilh's work are often treated stereotypically, and this one, queen of Thebes notwithstanding, is no exception, with her good works and petty bourgeois taste in furnishings. W.D. Howarth pertinently suggests that Anouilh's invention of these anachronisms is an 'unwarranted trivialisation' of what happens in the original scene in Sophocles, in which there is nothing to detract from the stoic dignity of the Queen's death and the stark simplicity of its narration. Anouilh leaves his signature in black ink in this scene in contriving for Eurydice such a caricaturally 'bourgeois' preoccupation with finishing her row of knitting before proceeding to the incongruous horror of cutting her throat.

60   *It's been a hard day*:   an understatement, *litotes*, to put it mildly. This figure of speech is one that the French often associate with the English mentality, but it is far from unknown in French culture too, and not inappropriate to Anouilh's bleak view of the world. His original French text here, with due change of tense, would recall for many members of the audience the famous *mot* of the eighteenth-century culprit Damiens as he prepared himself for the ordeal of being hanged, drawn and quartered: *la journée sera rude*.

60   *best never to grow up*:   Creon has lost his son and his wife in brutal suicides because Antigone could not grow up, yet it is sympathetically, and not with bitterness, that he refers to her in this closing reflection.

60   *But now it's over*:   at the end of Sophocles' *Antigone* the closing focus is similarly on Creon. But whereas Anouilh's Creon has been

exonerated, Sophocles' is in abject despair,
commonly held to be responsible for the tragedy
through his own pride, and admitting that he has
'killed unwittingly' his son and wife.
Appropriately, the Chorus's final words in
Sophocles are cathartic, and worth quoting in full:

> The key to human happiness
> Is to nurture wisdom in your heart,
> For man to attend to man's business
> And let the gods play their part:
> Above all, to stand in awe
> Of the eternal, unalterable law.
> The proud man may pretend
> In his arrogance to despise
> Everything but himself. In the end
> The gods will bring him to grief.
> Today it has happened here. With our own eyes
> We have seen an old man, through suffering,
>   become wise.
> (*Antigone* in *Sophocles Plays: One*, translated
>   by Don Taylor, p.188)

In Anouilh there is no such lesson to be learned.
There are only a number of observations to be
made by the Chorus: the bodies are rotting, their
names are being forgotten, Creon is waiting for
death and the guards carry on with their game of
cards in indifference to the day's events. In a
'Black Play' written at the height of the Second
World War, the innocence of the page is a small
miracle, and it is the best we can hope for.

Questions for Further Study

1. Can *Antigone* be interpreted simply as a clash between idealism and realism?

2. How helpful is it to interpret *Antigone* in the context of the occupation of France in the Second World War and French collaboration with the Germans?

3. Analyse Anouilh's deliberate use of anachronisms in the play and assess their usefulness for an understanding of the play's message.

4. 'The real hero of the play is Creon' (Charles Méré). Do you agree?

5. 'She wanted to die . . . Polynices was only an excuse.' Is this view of Antigone by Creon correct in your opinion?

6. 'Ismene, Eurydice, the nurse – Anouilh's picture of "normal" femininity is hardly flattering to the female half of the human race.' Do you agree?

7. Analyse the picture of the common people in *Antigone* (both in characters and in descriptions). How does it affect your interpretation of the play?

8. 'The healthy and radiant characters of Ismene and Haemon count for nothing in the end. Anouilh's vision of life could not be more misanthropic and his play is quite naturally in its right place among his "Black" series.' Discuss.

9. Analyse the letter scene at the end of *Antigone* and assess its significance.

10. 'The final confrontation between Antigone and Creon is a masterpiece of dramatic construction.' Do you agree?

11. Many critics of *Antigone*, particularly French ones, reproached Anouilh for his sentimentality (animals, the nurse, the page, childhood, toys, etc.). Discuss this aspect of the play and say whether you agree it has a negative effect.

12. '*Antigone* is first and foremost about the unbearable pain (experienced by one individual) of passing from adolescence to adulthood. This inevitably reduces its impact as a call to heroic resistance to tyranny.' Do you agree?

13. What conclusions do you draw from the fact that the German censors found no reason for banning performances of *Antigone* during the Second World War?

14. 'Anouilh clearly has no illusions about the human race in *Antigone*. So the spectator must have doubts about the cause Antigone is dying for, and thus doubts about her status as a tragic heroine.' Discuss.

15. Albert Camus said that the ideal balance for a dramatist handling the Antigone theme is one in which 'Antigone is right, but Creon is not wrong'. Do you believe Anouilh has achieved this in his play?

16. 'Anouilh's *Antigone* is similar to Sophocles' version in its plot but totally different in its philosophical and moral meaning.' Discuss.

17. Compare *Antigone* with any other play(s) by Anouilh with which you are familiar regarding the author's handling of themes and characterisation.

18. Compare *Antigone* with any other play(s) by modern French dramatists using Greek myths. Do you think this dramatic device can still succeed in our time?

19. Write a critique of any performance of *Antigone* you have seen, analysing in particular any artistic problems inherent in the play itself.

20. If you directed a modern production of *Antigone* how would you seek to make the play significant for audiences in the age in which we live?

21. 'Brecht's *Antigone* – now *there's* a play about resistance to tyranny.' Compare and discuss.

22. Anouilh's *Antigone*, in French or in translation, is always being performed somewhere in the world today. How do you account for this popularity?

Bloomsbury Methuen Drama Student Editions

Jean Anouilh *Antigone* • John Arden *Serjeant Musgrave's Dance*
Alan Ayckbourn *Confusions* • Aphra Behn *The Rover* • Edward Bond
Lear • *Saved* • Bertolt Brecht *The Caucasian Chalk Circle* • *Fear and
Misery in the Third Reich* • *The Good Person of Szechwan* • *Life of Galileo* •
Mother Courage and her Children • *The Resistible Rise of Arturo Ui* • *The
Threepenny Opera* • Anton Chekhov *The Cherry Orchard* • *The Seagull* •
Three Sisters • *Uncle Vanya* • Caryl Churchill *Serious Money* • *Top Girls*
• Shelagh Delaney *A Taste of Honey* • Euripides *Elektra* • *Medea*•
Dario Fo *Accidental Death of an Anarchist* • Michael Frayn *Copenhagen*
• John Galsworthy *Strife* • Nikolai Gogol *The Government Inspector* •
Robert Holman *Across Oka* • Henrik Ibsen *A Doll's House* • *Ghosts*•
Hedda Gabler • Charlotte Keatley *My Mother Said I Never Should* •
Bernard Kops *Dreams of Anne Frank* • Federico García Lorca *Blood
Wedding* • *Doña Rosita the Spinster* (bilingual edition) •*The House of
Bernarda Alba* • (bilingual edition) • *Yerma* (bilingual edition) • David
Mamet *Glengarry Glen Ross* • *Oleanna* • Patrick Marber *Closer* • John
Marston *Malcontent* • Martin McDonagh *The Lieutenant of Inishmore* •
Joe Orton *Loot* • Luigi Pirandello *Six Characters in Search of an Author*
• Mark Ravenhill *Shopping and F***ing* • Willy Russell *Blood Brothers*
• *Educating Rita* • Sophocles *Antigone* • *Oedipus the King* • Wole
Soyinka *Death and the King's Horseman* • Shelagh Stephenson *The
Memory of Water* • August Strindberg *Miss Julie* • J. M. Synge *The
Playboy of the Western World* • Theatre Workshop *Oh What a Lovely
War* Timberlake Wertenbaker *Our Country's Good* • Arnold Wesker
The Merchant • Oscar Wilde *The Importance of Being Earnest* •
Tennessee Williams *A Streetcar Named Desire* • *The Glass Menagerie*

Bloomsbury Methuen Drama World Classics

include

Jean Anouilh (two volumes)
Brendan Behan
Aphra Behn
Bertolt Brecht (eight volumes)
Büchner
Bulgakov
Calderón
Čapek
Anton Chekhov
Noël Coward (eight volumes)
Feydeau (two volumes)
Eduardo De Filippo
Max Frisch
John Galsworthy
Gogol
Gorky (two volumes)
Harley Granville Barker
   (two volumes)
Victor Hugo
Henrik Ibsen (six volumes)
Jarry

Lorca (three volumes)
Marivaux
Mustapha Matura
David Mercer (two volumes)
Arthur Miller (six volumes)
Molière
Musset
Peter Nichols (two volumes)
Joe Orton
A. W. Pinero
Luigi Pirandello
Terence Rattigan
   (two volumes)
W. Somerset Maugham
   (two volumes)
August Strindberg
   (three volumes)
J. M. Synge
Ramón del Valle-Inclán
Frank Wedekind
Oscar Wilde

Bloomsbury Methuen Drama Contemporary Dramatists

include

John Arden (two volumes)
Arden & D'Arcy
Peter Barnes (three volumes)
Sebastian Barry
Dermot Bolger
Edward Bond (eight volumes)
Howard Brenton
  (two volumes)
Richard Cameron
Jim Cartwright
Caryl Churchill (two volumes)
Sarah Daniels (two volumes)
Nick Darke
David Edgar (three volumes)
David Eldridge
Ben Elton
Dario Fo (two volumes)
Michael Frayn (three volumes)
David Greig
John Godber (four volumes)
Paul Godfrey
John Guare
Lee Hall (two volumes)
Peter Handke
Jonathan Harvey
  (two volumes)
Declan Hughes
Terry Johnson (three volumes)
Sarah Kane
Barrie Keeffe
Bernard-Marie Koltès
  (two volumes)
Franz Xaver Kroetz
David Lan
Bryony Lavery
Deborah Levy
Doug Lucie

David Mamet (four volumes)
Martin McDonagh
Duncan McLean
Anthony Minghella
  (two volumes)
Tom Murphy (six volumes)
Phyllis Nagy
Anthony Nellsen (two volumes)
Philip Osment
Gary Owen
Louise Page
Stewart Parker (two volumes)
Joe Penhall (two volumes)
Stephen Poliakoff
  (three volumes)
David Rabe (two volumes)
Mark Ravenhill (two volumes)
Christina Reid
Philip Ridley
Willy Russell
Eric-Emmanuel Schmitt
Ntozake Shange
Sam Shepard (two volumes)
Wole Soyinka (two volumes)
Simon Stephens (two volumes)
Shelagh Stephenson
David Storey (three volumes)
Sue Townsend
Judy Upton
Michel Vinaver
  (two volumes)
Arnold Wesker (two volumes)
Michael Wilcox
Roy Williams (three volumes)
Snoo Wilson (two volumes)
David Wood (two volumes)
Victoria Wood

Bloomsbury Methuen Drama Classical Greek Dramatists

Aeschylus Plays: One
(Persians, Seven Against Thebes, Suppliants,
Prometheus Bound)

Aeschylus Plays: Two
(Oresteia: Agamemnon, Libation-Bearers, Eumenides)

Aristophanes Plays: One
(Acharnians, Knights, Peace, Lysistrata)

Aristophanes Plays: Two
(Wasps, Clouds, Birds, Festival Time, Frogs)

Aristophanes & Menander: New Comedy
(Women in Power, Wealth, The Malcontent,
The Woman from Samos)

Euripides Plays: One
(Medea, The Phoenician Women, Bacchae)

Euripides Plays: Two
(Hecuba, The Women of Troy, Iphigeneia at Aulis,
Cyclops)

Euripides Plays: Three
(Alkestis, Helen, Ion)

Euripides Plays: Four
(Elektra, Orestes, Iphigeneia in Tauris)

Euripides Plays: Five
(Andromache, Herakles' Children, Herakles)

Euripides Plays: Six
(Hippolytos, Suppliants, Rhesos)

Sophocles Plays: One
(Oedipus the King, Oedipus at Colonus, Antigone)

Sophocles Plays: Two
(Ajax, Women of Trachis, Electra, Philoctetes)